Kaplan Publishing are constantly finding ne~ looking for exam success and our online re extra dimension to your studies.

C000184349

This book comes with free MyKaplan online resou~ study anytime, anywhere. **This free online resource is not sol~ separately and is included in the price of the book.**

Having purchased this book, you have access to the following online study materials:

CONTENT	AAT	
	Text	Kit
Electronic version of the book	✓	✓
Knowledge Check tests with instant answers	✓	
Mock assessments online	✓	✓
Material updates	✓	✓

How to access your online resources

Received this book as part of your Kaplan course?
If you have a MyKaplan account, your full online resources will be added automatically, in line with the information in your course confirmation email. If you've not used MyKaplan before, you'll be sent an activation email once your resources are ready.

Bought your book from Kaplan?
We'll automatically add your online resources to your MyKaplan account. If you've not used MyKaplan before, you'll be sent an activation email.

Bought your book from elsewhere?
Go to **www.mykaplan.co.uk/add-online-resources**
Enter the ISBN number found on the title page and back cover of this book.
Add the unique pass key number contained in the scratch panel below.
You may be required to enter additional information during this process to set up or confirm your account details.

This code can only be used once for the registration of this book online. This registration and your online content will expire when the examinations covered by this book have taken place. Please allow one hour from the time you submit your book details for us to process your request.

Please scratch the film to access your unique code.

Please be aware that this code is case-sensitive and you will need to include the dashes within the passcode, but not when entering the ISBN.

KAPLAN

PUBLISHING

AAT

Q2022

Financial Accounting: Preparing Financial Statements

EXAM KIT

This Exam Kit supports study for the following AAT qualifications:
AAT Level 3 Diploma in Accounting
AAT Level 3 Certificate in Bookkeeping
AAT Diploma in Accounting at SCQF Level 7

PUBLISHING

British Library Cataloguing-in-Publication Data

A catalogue record for this book is available from the British Library.

Published by:

Kaplan Publishing UK

Unit 2 The Business Centre

Molly Millar's Lane

Wokingham

Berkshire

RG41 2QZ

ISBN: 978-1-83996-585-2

© Kaplan Financial Limited, 2023

Printed and bound in Great Britain.

CONTENTS

Features in this exam kit

In addition to providing a wide ranging bank of real exam style questions, we have also included in this kit:

- unit-specific information and advice on exam technique

- our recommended approach to make your revision for this particular unit as effective as possible.

You will find a wealth of other resources to help you with your studies on the AAT website:

www.aat.org.uk/

Quality and accuracy are of the utmost importance to us so if you spot an error in any of our products, please send an email to mykaplanreporting@kaplan.com with full details, or follow the link to the feedback form in MyKaplan.

Our Quality Co-ordinator will work with our technical team to verify the error and take action to ensure it is corrected in future editions.

UNIT-SPECIFIC INFORMATION

THE EXAM

FORMAT OF THE ASSESSMENT

The assessment will comprise six independent tasks. Students will be assessed by computer-based assessment.

In any one assessment, students may not be assessed on all content, or on the full depth or breadth of a piece of content. The content assessed may change over time to ensure validity of assessment, but all assessment criteria will be tested over time.

The learning outcomes for this unit are as follows:

	Learning outcome	Weighting
1	Understand the accounting principles underlying final accounts preparation	5%
2	Understand the principles of advanced double-entry bookkeeping	10%
3	Implement procedures for the acquisition and disposal of non-current assets	10%
4	Prepare and record depreciation calculations	10%
5	Record period end adjustments	10%
6	Produce and extend the trial balance	15%
7	Produce the financial statements for sole traders and partnerships	20%
8	Interpret financial statements using profitability ratios	10%
9	Prepare accounting records from incomplete information	10%
	Total	100%

Time allowed

2 ½ hours

PASS MARK

The pass mark for all AAT CBAs is 70%.

 Always keep your eye on the clock and make sure you attempt all questions!

DETAILED SYLLABUS

The detailed syllabus and study guide written by the AAT can be found at:

www.aat.org.uk/

INDEX TO QUESTIONS AND ANSWERS

EXAM TECHNIQUE

- **Do not skip any of the material** in the syllabus.

- **Read each question** *very* carefully.

- **Double-check your answer** before committing yourself to it.

- Answer **every** question – if you do not know an answer to a multiple choice question or true/false question, you don't lose anything by guessing. Think carefully before you **guess**.

- If you are answering a multiple-choice question, **eliminate first those answers that you know are wrong.** Then choose the most appropriate answer from those that are left.

- **Don't panic** if you realise you've answered a question incorrectly. Getting one question wrong will not mean the difference between passing and failing.

Computer-based exams – tips

- Do not attempt a CBA until you have **completed all study material** relating to it.

- On the AAT website there is a CBA demonstration. It is **ESSENTIAL** that you attempt this before your real CBA. You will become familiar with how to move around the CBA screens and the way that questions are formatted, increasing your confidence and speed in the actual exam.

- Be sure you understand how to use the **software** before you start the exam. If in doubt, ask the assessment centre staff to explain it to you.

- Questions are **displayed on the screen** and answers are entered using keyboard and mouse. At the end of the exam, you are given a certificate showing the result you have achieved.

- In addition to the traditional multiple-choice question type, CBAs will also contain **other types of questions**, such as number entry questions, drag and drop, true/false, pick lists or drop down menus or hybrids of these.

- In some CBAs you will have to type in complete computations or written answers.

- You need to be sure you **know how to answer questions** of this type before you sit the exam, through practice.

KAPLAN'S RECOMMENDED REVISION APPROACH

QUESTION PRACTICE IS THE KEY TO SUCCESS

Success in professional examinations relies upon you acquiring a firm grasp of the required knowledge at the tuition phase. In order to be able to do the questions, knowledge is essential.

However, the difference between success and failure often hinges on your exam technique on the day and making the most of the revision phase of your studies.

The **Kaplan Study Text** is the starting point, designed to provide the underpinning knowledge to tackle all questions. However, in the revision phase, poring over text books is not the answer.

Kaplan Pocket Notes are designed to help you quickly revise a topic area; however you then need to practise questions. There is a need to progress to exam style questions as soon as possible, and to tie your exam technique and technical knowledge together.

The importance of question practice cannot be over-emphasised.

The recommended approach below is designed by expert tutors in the field, in conjunction with their knowledge of the examiner and the specimen assessment.

You need to practise as many questions as possible in the time you have left.

OUR AIM

Our aim is to get you to the stage where you can attempt exam questions confidently, to time, in a closed book environment, with no supplementary help (i.e. to simulate the real examination experience).

Practising your exam technique is also vitally important for you to assess your progress and identify areas of weakness that may need more attention in the final run up to the examination.

In order to achieve this we recognise that initially you may feel the need to practice some questions with open book help.

Good exam technique is vital.

THE KAPLAN REVISION PLAN

Stage 1: Assess areas of strengths and weaknesses

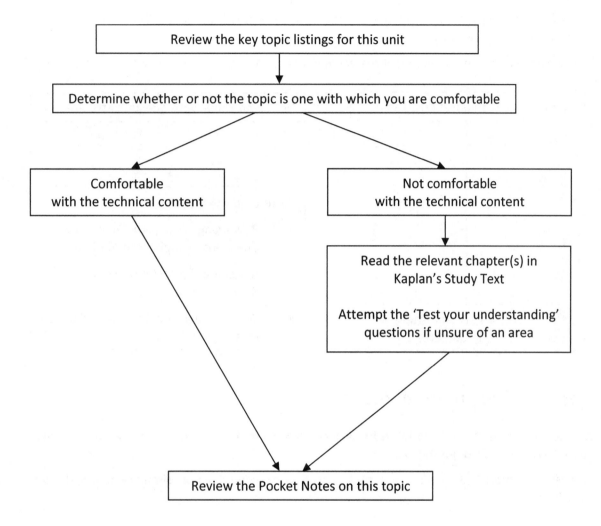

Stage 2: Practice questions

Follow the order of revision of topics as presented in this Kit and attempt the questions in the order suggested.

Try to avoid referring to Study Texts and your notes and the model answer until you have completed your attempt.

Review your attempt with the model answer and assess how much of the answer you achieved.

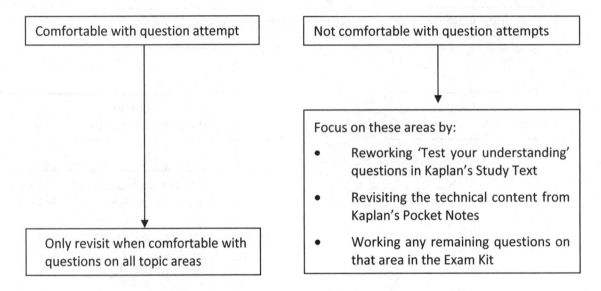

Stage 3: Final pre-exam revision

We recommend that you **attempt at least one mock examination** containing a set of previously unseen exam-standard questions.

Attempt the mock CBA online in timed, closed book conditions to simulate the real exam experience.

Section 1

PRACTICE QUESTIONS

UNDERSTAND THE ACCOUNTING PRINCIPLES UNDERLYING FINAL ACCOUNTS PREPARATION

1 MULTIPLE CHOICE QUESTIONS

Choose ONE answer from each part.

1 **Which one of the following concepts explains why we sometimes post prepayment adjustments in the accounts?**

   A   The going concern concept

   B   The prepayments concept

   C   The accruals concept

   D   The prudence concept

2 **What is the missing word from the definition of asset provided?**

   'An asset is a resource _____ by the entity as a result of past events and from which future economic benefits are expected to flow to the entity.'

   A   Owned

   B   Used

   C   Recognised

   D   Controlled

3 **Which of the following is the correct accounting equation?**

   A   Non-current assets + Current assets = current liabilities + Long term liabilities

   B   Assets + Liabilities = Capital – Profit + Drawings

   C   Assets – Liabilities = Capital + Profit – Drawings

   D   Capital = Profit – drawings

4 **A business buys a non-current asset on credit. Which elements of the accounting equation will be affected by this transaction?**

   A   Assets only

   B   Assets and liabilities only

   C   Assets and capital only

   D   Assets, liabilities and capital

5   A business with a large positive bank balance sends a cheque to a supplier of its inventory items, to settle part of the balance due to the supplier. Which elements of the accounting equation will be affected by this transaction?

A   Assets only

B   Assets and liabilities only

C   Assets and capital only

D   Assets, liabilities and capital

6   Which of the following is correct regarding the closing balance on a ledger account?

1   A credit balance exists where total credits exceed total debits

2   A credit balance exists where total debits exceed total credits

3   A debit balance exists where total debits exceed total credits

4   A debit balance exists where total credits exceed total debits

A   1 and 4 only

B   All of them

C   1 and 3 only

D   2 and 3 only

7   Which ONE of the following is the correct entry to record the purchase on credit of inventory intended for resale?

A   Debit inventory, credit receivable

B   Debit inventory, credit payable

C   Debit purchases, credit payable

D   Debit payable, credit purchases

8   The double-entry system of bookkeeping normally results in which of the following balances on the ledger accounts?

A   **Debit:** Assets and revenues **Credit:** Liabilities, capital and expenses

B   **Debit:** Revenues, capital and liabilities **Credit:** Assets and expenses

C   **Debit:** Assets and expenses **Credit:** Liabilities, capital and revenues

D   **Debit:** Assets, expenses and capital **Credit:** Liabilities and revenues

9   Which ONE of the following should be classified as a non-current asset?

A   A car purchased for resale by a car dealer

B   A positive bank account (debit)

C   A car for use by the company salesman

D   An insurance invoice covering the following 12 month period

10   Which ONE of the following should be classified as a current liability?

A   An item of inventory that will be sold in the next couple of months

B   A delivery van that will be sold next week

C   A loan that will be paid back to the bank in the next few months

D   A sales invoice for goods sold to a customer that will be paid in the next month

2   USERS OF THE FINAL ACCOUNTS

Link the users of final accounts on the left below with the most likely reason for their interest on the right.

To make decisions regarding their investment

HMRC

To assess the security of any loan

Shareholders

To compare information from other organisations operating in the same sector

To assess the amount of tax payable by the business

3   THE FUNDAMENTAL QUALITATIVE CHARACTERISTICS

From the list below select the TWO fundamental qualitative characteristics of useful financial information.

	✓
Faithful representation	
Objectivity	
Communication	
Relevance	
Comparability	
Understandability	

4   BORIS

You have worked on the accounts of Boris, a sole trader, for many years. In the last 5 years, Boris has made some quite substantial losses.

Based on this information, which ONE of the following accounting concepts require particular consideration when preparing the final accounts of Boris?

	✓
Accruals	
Going concern	
Consistency	
None of the above	

5 INTERNATIONAL ACCOUNTING STANDARDS

Match each of the following International Accounting Standards with the relevant accounting rule.

	IAS 2 ✓	IAS 16 ✓
Property, plant and equipment is measured at its cost and depreciated so that its depreciable amount is allocated over its useful life.		
Inventories should be valued at the lower of cost and net realisable value.		

6 USERS AND QUALITIES OF FINANCIAL INFORMATION

This task is about interpreting financial statements using profitability ratios.

(a) (i) Identify which TWO of the following are considered primary users of final accounts.

	✓
Current shareholders	
Customers	
Government	
Competitors	
Lenders	

(ii) Identify whether the following qualities of useful financial information are considered to be fundamental or enhancing qualities as per the Conceptual Framework.

Definition	Fundamental ✓	Enhancing ✓
Verifiability		
Relevance		
Comparability		
Faithful representation		

7   ACCOUNTING PRINCIPLES AND QUALITATIVE CHARACTERISTICS I

(a)   (i)   Identify the accounting principle described in each of the following scenarios.

Scenario	Principle
The business recognises the costs of using a broadband connection during the period despite having not been billed by the network provider.	PICKLIST
Jiaoming owns and runs a gym and takes a set of dumbbells home for own use. This is recorded as drawings.	PICKLIST
Stationery items such as staplers are treated as expenses rather than as non-current assets.	PICKLIST
The business presents non-current assets and non-current liabilities separately in the statement of financial position.	PICKLIST

PICKLIST
Accruals principle
Business entity principle
Materiality principle
Going concern principle

(ii)   Match the definition of each of the enhancing qualitative characteristics of useful financial information with the term from the picklist.

Definition	Term
When knowledgeable and independent observers reach a consensus that the information presented is faithfully represented.	PICKLIST
Providing information to decision makers at a point that will make it capable of influencing their economic decisions.	PICKLIST

PICKLIST
Relevance
Faithful representation
Comparability
Verifiability
Timeliness
Understandability

8   ACCOUNTING PRINCIPLES AND CHARACTERISTICS II

(a)   (i)   Identify the accounting principle described in each of the following scenarios.

Scenario	Principle
Accounting policies should not be changed regularly from one year to the next, unless the change provides a more true and fair view.	PICKLIST
Income received in advance is recorded as deferred income in the statement of financial position until the service is provided at a future date, at which point the income is recorded in the statement of profit or loss.	PICKLIST
The owners of a business take a mobile phone from their business' supplies to give to their daughter for her birthday and record this as drawings	PICKLIST
The business presents non-current assets and non-current liabilities separately in the statement of financial position.	PICKLIST

PICKLIST
Accruals principle
Business entity principle
Materiality
Going concern
Consistency
Prudence

(ii)   Identify each of the qualitative characteristics of useful financial information as described below.

Scenario	Qualitative characteristic
Providing information that is complete, neutral and free from error.	PICKLIST
Classifying, characterising and presenting information clearly and concisely.	PICKLIST

PICKLIST
Relevance
Faithful representation
Comparability
Verifiability
Timeliness
Understandability

9 ACCOUNTING PRINCIPLES I

(a) (i) Identify which TWO of the following are considered fundamental qualitative characteristics of financial information.

	✓
Verifiability	
Accruals	
Faithful representation	
Going concern	
Relevance	

(ii) Identify the accounting principle being described in each of the following definitions.

Definition	Accounting principle
Sales revenue should be recognised when goods and services have been supplied; costs are incurred when goods and services have been received	PICKLIST
Financial statements are produced using the assumption that a business will remain in business for the foreseeable future.	PICKLIST
Transactions and valuation methods are treated the same way from year to year. This means that users of accounts can, therefore, make more meaningful comparisons of financial performance from year to year.	PICKLIST
Expenses are included in the accounts as soon as there is a reasonable chance that such costs will be incurred in the future.	PICKLIST

PICKLIST
Accruals principle
Business entity principle
Materiality
Going concern
Consistency
Prudence

10 FINANCIAL STATEMENTS

(i) Complete the following statement.

The financial statements are produced by .....PICKLIST...... so that .....PICKLIST...... can assess the financial performance of the business

PICKLIST
the directors
the users

(ii) Identify each of the following items as either an accounting concept or a qualitative characteristic of useful financial information.

Definition	Accounting concept or qualitative characteristic
Understandability	PICKLIST
Relevance	PICKLIST
Going Concern	PICKLIST
Accruals	PICKLIST

PICKLIST
Accounting concept
Qualitative characteristic

11   ACCOUNTING PRINCIPLES II

(a)   (i)   Identify the accounting principle described in each of the following scenarios.

Scenario	Principle
From one year to the next, a business uses the same approach to calculate its depreciation and its allowance for doubtful receivables.	PICKLIST
A business records an allowance for doubtful receivables against its receivables despite there still being a chance of receiving the outstanding amount.	PICKLIST
A payment made to a supplier for services that will be received in the next accounting period will be recorded as a prepayment.	PICKLIST
Capital purchases with a value lower than a certain threshold set by the owners can be written off directly to the profit or loss as an expense.	PICKLIST

PICKLIST
Accruals principle
Business entity principle
Materiality
Consistency
Prudence

(ii)   Identify whether each of the following statements is true or false.

Statement	True ✓	False ✓
Relevance is an enhancing qualitative characteristic of useful financial information		
The lenders of a business are considered one of the primary users of the financial statements		

12 USERS OF FINAL ACCOUNTS

(a) (i) Identify which TWO of the following are considered primary users of final accounts.

	✓
Current shareholders	
Customers	
Lenders	
Competitors	
Management	

(ii) Identify whether each of the following qualities of useful financial information are considered as fundamental or enhancing characteristics as per the Conceptual Framework.

Definition	Fundamental or enhancing
Verifiability	PICKLIST
Faithful representation	PICKLIST
Comparability	PICKLIST
Understandability	PICKLIST

PICKLIST
Fundamental
Enhancing

UNDERSTAND THE PRINCIPLES OF ADVANCED DOUBLE-ENTRY BOOKKEEPING

13 MULTIPLE CHOICE QUESTIONS

Choose ONE answer from each part.

1 **Which of the following changes could NOT occur as a result of an entry in the bookkeeping records?**

A   Increase asset and increase liability

B   Increase asset and increase capital

C   Increase capital and increase liability

D   Increase capital and decrease liability

2   A business has capital of £10,000 and liabilities of £4,000.

   Which of the following asset and liability figures could appear in this business' statement of financial position?

   A   Assets £6,000   Liabilities   £16,000

   B   Assets£6,000   Liabilities   £4,000

   C   Assets£10,000   Liabilities   £10,000

   D   Assets£14,000   Liabilities   £4,000

3   **A debit balance would be expected to arise when the accounts are balanced at the period end on which of the following accounts?**

   A   Capital

   B   Sales

   C   Electricity

   D   Loan

4   **A credit balance would be expected to arise when the accounts are balanced at the period end on which of the following accounts?**

   A   Drawings

   B   Telephone

   C   Receivables

   D   Payables

5   **Which of the following describes the separate entity principle?**

   A   The assets of a business are a separate entity from the liabilities

   B   The drawings of a business are a separate entity from the profit of the business

   C   The business is a separate entity from the owner of the business

   D   The owner of the business must be a separate entity from a lender to the business

6   **Which of the following is a liability?**

   A   Trade receivables

   B   Inventory

   C   Bank overdraft

   D   Drawings

7   **Which of the following is NOT an asset?**

   A   Owner's capital

   B   Petty cash

   C   Salesman's motor car

   D   Computer software

14 DOUBLE-ENTRY

For each of the transactions below, tick whether the account balance would be debited, credited or would not change. Choose ONE answer for each line.

(a)   A sole trader makes a credit sale (ignore VAT)

	Debit	Credit	No change
Revenue			
Loan			
Non-current assets			
Trade receivables			

(b)   A sole trader decides to write off an irrecoverable debt

	Debit	Credit	No change
Trade payables			
Inventory			
Irrecoverable debt expense			
Trade receivables			

(c)   A sole trader purchases a new computer on credit for use in the business

	Debit	Credit	No change
Discount allowed			
Sundry payables			
Non-current assets			
Inventory			

(d)   A sole trader accounts for the cash received on disposal of a motor vehicle

	Debit	Credit	No change
Motor vehicles repairs			
Motor vehicles depreciation expense			
Disposal of motor vehicles account			
Bank			

(e)   A sole trader pays transport costs to have goods delivered to the premises of the business

	Debit	Credit	No change
Bank			
Carriage inwards			
Carriage outwards			
Purchases			

(f)   A sole trader pays transport costs to have goods delivered to customers

	Debit	Credit	No change
Bank			
Carriage inwards			
Carriage outwards			
Sales			

15   CLASSIFYING TRANSACTIONS AND BALANCES

Listed below are a number of transactions and balances that may be common to many businesses.

Fill in the boxes to indicate whether the items are assets, liabilities, expenses or income.

(a)   Goods stored in the warehouse awaiting resale

(b)   Electricity bill paid

(c)   Cash received from sale of goods

(d)   Amounts owing from a customer

(e)   Rent paid for the factory building

(f)   Cash paid into the business by the owner

(g)   Amounts owed to suppliers

(h)   Cash held in the till

(i)   Machinery purchased for use in the factory

(j)   Rent received for subletting part of the factory premises

(k)   Cash held in the business bank account

16   BILL SMITH – ACCOUNTING EQUATION

In the following transactions the accounting equation builds up at each stage.

Use the boxes below the accounting equation to show the amounts in each category in which the transactions would be recorded and what the business owns and owes cumulatively, after each transaction.

(a)   Bill Smith starts a new business by putting £10,000 into a business bank account.

Assets =	Capital	+ Profit	– Drawings	+ Liabilities

(b)   A bank lends the business a further £5,000.

Assets =	Capital	+ Profit	– Drawings	+ Liabilities

(c)   Bill buys a delivery van for £6,000.

Assets =	Capital	+ Profit	– Drawings	+ Liabilities

(d)   Bill buys inventory for £2,500 by writing out a business cheque.

Assets =	Capital	+ Profit	– Drawings	+ Liabilities

(e)   All the inventory is sold for £4,000. The money is paid direct to the business bank account.

(Remember there are two elements to this transaction. Firstly, the money coming into the business and the fact that the business no longer has an inventory asset, and secondly, the calculation of profit.)

Assets =	Capital	+ Profit	– Drawings	+ Liabilities

(f)   Bill pays a business expense of £400 out of the business bank account.

Assets =	Capital	+ Profit	– Drawings	+ Liabilities

(g)   Finally Bill takes £300 out of the business for his own purposes.

Assets =	Capital	+ Profit	– Drawings	+ Liabilities

17   ASSETS OR LIABILITIES

Given below is a list of typical assets and liabilities that might be found in a business.

Required:

Fill in the boxes by stating whether each of the following items is either an asset or a liability.

(a)   Cars for use by the sales team

(b)   Computers for resale

(c)   Bank overdraft

(d)   Monies owed by a customer

(e)   Trade payables

(f)   Office furniture

(g)   Trade receivables

18   TERMINOLOGY

Fill in the gaps to identify the following terms:

(a)   An .... is a present resource controlled by the .... as a result of a past...............

(b)   A ....is an amount owed by the business to another business or individual.

Examples include a .... and amounts owed to the suppliers of goods or services which have yet to be paid for.

(c)   .... is an asset comprising goods purchased for resale, components for inclusion in manufactured products, and the finished products which have been manufactured which have not yet been sold.

(d)   .... is the liability of the business to the owner of the business.

(e)   .... is the term which refers to amounts taken out of the business by the owner.

19   ALI

Ali's business had cash at bank of £1,780 on 1 June 20X4.

What was Ali's cash at bank balance at 30 June 20X4 after accounting for the following transactions in June?

1   Ali withdrew £200 per week to cover living expenses.

2   A customer paid for goods with a list price of £600, less trade discount of 5%.

3   An amount of £400 was received from a credit customer.

4   Banking's of £1,200 from canteen vending machines.

£

20   MIN

You are helping to prepare the financial statements of Min for the year ended 30 April 20X5. There are a number of accounting issues to deal with before the financial statements can be finalised.

Task 1

During the year, problems were experienced with goods from a particular supplier. In total, goods which cost £300,000, inclusive of VAT at 20%, were returned to the supplier.

State the accounting entries required to record the return of goods to the supplier.

	£000	Credit/Debit
Revenue		
Returns inwards		
Returns outwards		
VAT		
Trade payables' ledger control account		
Trade receivables'' ledger control account		

Task 2

During the year, Min withdrew goods from the business for his personal use. The goods cost £15,000 and had a sale value of £20,000.

State the accounting entries required to record withdrawal of goods from the business by Min for personal use.

	£000	Credit/Debit
Drawings		
Trade payables' ledger control account		
Purchases		
Revenue		

ACCOUNTING FOR AND MONITORING NON-CURRENT ASSETS

21   MULTIPLE CHOICE QUESTIONS

Choose ONE answer from each part.

1   **Which one of the following should be accounted for as capital expenditure?**

   A   The cost of painting a building

   B   The replacement of windows in a building

   C   The purchase of a car by a garage for resale

   D   Legal fees incurred on the purchase of a building

2   An organisation's non-current assets register shows a carrying amount of £135,600. The non-current asset account in the general ledger shows a carrying amount of £125,600. Which ONE of the following could explain this difference?

   A   The difference could be due to a disposed asset not having been deducted from the non-current assets register with disposal proceeds of £15,000 and a profit on disposal of £5,000

   B   The difference could be due to a disposed asset not having been deducted from the non-current assets register with disposal proceeds of £15,000 and a carrying amount of £5,000

   C   The difference could be due to a disposed asset not having been deducted from the non-current assets register with disposal proceeds of £15,000 and a loss on disposal of £5,000

   D   The difference could be due to a disposed asset not having been deducted from the non-current assets register with disposal proceeds of £5,000 and a carrying amount of £5,000

3   Which ONE of the statements below is correct?

   A   A non-current asset register is an alternative name for the non-current asset ledger account

   B   A non-current asset register is a list of receivables and payables

   C   A non-current asset register is a schedule of planned maintenance of non-current assets for use by the plant engineer

   D   A non-current asset register is a schedule of the cost and other information about each individual non-current asset

4   What journal entry is required to correctly account for the depreciation charge for the year of £3,500 relating to buildings?

   A   Debit Depreciation expense £3,500, and Credit Buildings £3,500

   B   Debit Buildings £3,500, and Credit Accumulated depreciation £3,500

   C   Debit Depreciation expense £3,500 and Credit Accumulated depreciation £3,500

   D   Debit Accumulated depreciation £3,500, and Credit Depreciation expense £3,500

5   Which of the following statements is true in relation to the non-current asset register?

   A   It is an alternative name for the non-current asset ledger account.

   B   It is a list of the physical non-current assets rather than their financial cost.

   C   It is a schedule of planned maintenance of non-current assets for use by the plant engineer.

   D   It is a schedule of the cost and other information about each individual non-current asset.

6   A non-current asset was purchased at the beginning of Year 1 for £2,400 and depreciated at 20% per annum using the diminishing-balance method. At the beginning of Year 4 it was sold for £1,200.

What was the profit or loss on disposal?

A   £240.00 loss

B   £28.80 loss

C   £28.80 profit

D   £240.00 profit

7   W Co bought a new printing machine from abroad. The cost of the machine was £80,000. The installation costs were £5,000 and the employees received training on how to use the machine, at a cost of £2,000. Before using the machine to print customers' orders, pre-production safety testing was undertaken at a cost of £1,000.

What should be the cost of the machine in W Co's statement of financial position?

£ [   ]

8   A non-current asset was disposed of for £2,200 during the last accounting year. It had been purchased exactly three years earlier for £5,000, with a residual value of £500, and had been depreciated on the diminishing-balance basis, at 20% per annum.

What was the profit or loss on disposal?

A   £360 loss

B   £150 loss

C   £104 loss

D   £200 profit

9   **Which of the following items should be accounted for as asset expenditure?**

A   The cost of painting a building

B   The replacement of broken windows in a building

C   The purchase of a car by a car dealer for re-sale

D   Legal fees incurred on the purchase of a building

10   F Co purchased a car for £12,000 on 1 April 20X1 which has been depreciated at 20% each year straight-line, assuming no residual value. F Co's policy is to charge a full year's depreciation in the year of purchase and no depreciation in the year of sale. The car was traded in for a replacement vehicle on 1 August 20X4 for an agreed figure of £5,000.

What was the profit or loss on the disposal of the vehicle for the year ended 31 December 20X4?

A   Loss £2,200

B   Loss £1,400

C   Loss £200

D   Profit £200

22 SOUTHGATE TRADING

The following is a purchase invoice received by Southgate Trading, which is registered for VAT:

To: Southgate Trading Unit 26, Three Cliffs Trading Estate Gowerton GW14 6PW	Invoice 535 Computer Supplies plc 12 Hanger Lane Bedgrove	Date: 28 March X9	
			£
HP colour laser printer	Serial number 65438LKR	1	750.00
Delivery		1	25.00
Printer cartridges @ £20.00 each		2	40.00
VAT @ 20%			163.00
Total			978.00
Settlement terms: strictly 30 days net.			

The following information relates to the sale of a vehicle:

Registration number	AB 08 DRF
Date of sale	15 March X9
Selling price excluding VAT	£4,500.00

- Southgate Trading has a policy of capitalising expenditure over £500.
- Vehicles are depreciated at 25% on a diminishing-balance basis.
- Computer equipment is depreciated at 30% on a straight-line basis assuming no residual value.
- Non-current assets are depreciated in the year of acquisition but not in the year of disposal.

Record the following information in the non-current assets register below:

(a) any acquisitions of non-current assets during the year ended 31 March 20X9

(b) any disposals of non-current assets during the year ended 31 March 20X9

(c) depreciation for the year ended 31 March 20X9.

Non-current assets register

Description	Acquisition date	Cost £	Depreciation charges £	Carrying amount £	Funding method	Disposal proceeds	Disposal date
Computer equipment							
Server main office	30/09/X6	2,800.00			Cash		
Year end 31/03/X7			840.00	1,960.00			
Year end 31/03/X8			840.00	1,120.00			
Year end 31/03/X9							
Motor vehicles							
AB08 DRF	01/04/X6	12,000.00			Cash		
Year end 31/03/X7			3,000.00	9,000.00			
Year end 31/03/X8			2,250.00	6,750.00			
Year end 31/03/X9							
AB 07 FRP	31/01/X8	9,600.00			Cash		
Year end 31/03/X8			2,400.00	7,200.00			
Year end 31/03/X9							

(d) The main office has been rewired to accommodate the new computer equipment. The work carried out was completed by some employees of the business as opposed to external contractors. On the same day, the room was given a coat of paint to the new office manager's favourite colour – egg shell blue. The costs of the rewiring and the painting were:

Wages to rewire the room: £250

Materials to rewire the room: £410

Office re-paint: £100

What is the additional cost to be recorded as capital expenditure?

£_____

Note: You are not required to enter any additional capital expenditure from part (d) into the non-current assets register.

23 TK FABRICATIONS

The following is a purchase invoice received by TK Fabrications, who is registered for VAT:

Invoice 514		
To: TK Fabrications	Welding Wizards	**Date:** 28 January X9
Block 6	22 Springfield Grove	
Pipps Hill Industrial Estate	Southwold	
Southwold	ST8 4RY	
ST5 9PQ		
		£
Welding iron	Equipment no 289XP4	850.00
Delivery		15.00
Welding material pack		60.00
VAT @20%		185.00
Total		1,110.00
Settlement terms: strictly 30 days net		

The following information relates to the sale of a vehicle:

Registration number	PF07 THY
Date of sale	20 January X9
Selling price excluding VAT	£8,500.00

- TK Fabrications has a policy of capitalising expenditure over £500.
- Vehicles are depreciated at 25% on a diminishing-balance basis.
- Equipment is depreciated at 15% on a straight-line basis assuming no residual value.
- Non-current assets are depreciated in the year of acquisition but not in the year of disposal.

Record the following information in the non-current assets register below:

(a)   any acquisitions of non-current assets during the year ended 31 January X9

(b)   any disposals of non-current assets during the year ended 31 January X9

(c)   depreciation for the year ended 31 January X9.

Non-current assets register

Description	Acquisition date	Cost £	Depreciation charges £	Carrying amount £	Funding method	Disposal proceeds	Disposal date
Equipment							
Workshop fit out	17/07/X6	5,400.00			Cash		
Year end 31/01/X7			810.00	4,590.00			
Year end 31/01/X8			810.00	3,780.00			
Year end 31/01/X9							
Motor vehicles							
PF07 THY	04/06/X6	13,500.00			Cash		
Year end 31/01/X7			3,375.00	10,125.00			
Year end 31/01/X8			2,531.25	7,593.75			
Year end 31/01/X9							
SR08 EKE	24/01/X8	7,300.00			Part-exchange		
Year end 31/01/X8			1,825.00	5,475.00			
Year end 31/01/X9							

24   BYTES TECHNOLOGY GROUP

The following is a purchase invoice received by Bytes Technology Group, who is registered for VAT:

	Invoice 84297	
To: Bytes Technology Group 119 Abbots Close Petersfield PF10 1FR	PC Universe 13 Heron Drive Petersfield PF4 9QZ	**Date:** 28 March X9
		£
Printer	Serial number 1807G92	550.00
Delivery		10.00
Printer cartridges		40.00
VAT @20%		120.00
Total		720.00
Settlement terms: strictly 30 days net		

The following information relates to the sale of a vehicle:

Registration number	EJ09 TYZ
Date of sale	20 March X9
Selling price excluding VAT	£3,200.00

- Bytes Technology Group has a policy of capitalising expenditure over £500.
- Vehicles are depreciated at 30% on a diminishing-balance basis.
- Computer Equipment is depreciated at 20% on a straight-line basis assuming no residual value.
- Non-current assets are depreciated in the year of acquisition but not in the year of disposal.

Record the following information in the non-current assets register below:

(a)   any acquisitions of non-current assets during the year ended 31 March X9

(b)   any disposals of non-current assets during the year ended 31 March X9

(c)   depreciation for the year ended 31 March X9.

Non-current assets register

Description	Acquisition date	Cost £	Depreciation charges £	Carrying amount £	Funding method	Disposal proceeds	Disposal date
Computer equipment							
Mainframe Server	17/07/X6	14,000.00			Cash		
Year end 31/03/X7			2,800.00	11,200.00			
Year end 31/03/X8			2,800.00	8,400.00			
Year end 31/03/X9							
Motor vehicles							
EJ09 TYZ	14/09/X6	9,000.00			Cash		
Year end 31/03/X7			2,700.00	6,300.00			
Year end 31/03/X8			1,890.00	4,410.00			
Year end 31/03/X9							
EA55 SAR	12/02/X8	10,000.00			Part-exchange		
Year end 31/03/X8			3,000.00	7,000.00			
Year end 31/03/X9							

(d) Which of the following could be added to the non-current assets register to improve its usability?

	Tick
The colour of the asset	
The user of the assets	
The age of the asset	
The location of the asset	

25   JACO TRADING

You may ignore VAT in this task.

The following is a purchase invoice received by Jaco Trading, relating to new equipment for its pizza and pasta kitchen.

To: Jaco Trading Unit 32, Old Rome Estate Ayr KA8 1BB	**Invoice 75134** Pizza Equipment Armour Road Glasgow G14 7YT		**Date:** 01 April 20X7
Item	**Details**		**£**
Electric deck pizza oven	ERJ0506	1	3,565.00
Static stand	For ERJ0506	1	200.00
Aluminium blade pizza peel	EJL213	10	150.00
Net total			3,915.00

This acquisition has been made under a lease agreement.

The information that follows relates to the sale of some IT equipment which is no longer used by Jaco Trading.

Description of item:	Laptop 4911
Date of sale:	30 September 20X7
Selling price:	£200.00

- Jaco Trading has a policy of capitalising expenditure over £300.
- Kitchen equipment is depreciated at 25% on a diminishing-balance basis.
- Computer equipment is depreciated on a straight-line basis over 5 years assuming no residual value.
- Depreciation is calculated on an annual basis and charged in equal instalments for each full month an asset is owned in the year.

Record the following information in the extract of the non-current assets register below:

(a)   any acquisitions of non-current assets during the year ended 31 March X8

(b)   any disposals of non-current assets during the year ended 31 March X8

(c)   depreciation for the year ended 31 March X8.

Note: Not every cell with require an entry. Show numerical answers to TWO decimal places. Use the DD/MM/YY format for any dates.

Extract from the non-current assets register

Description	Acquisition date	Cost £	Depreciation charges £	Carrying amount £	Funding method	Disposal proceeds	Disposal date
Kitchen equipment							
American-style fridge freezer	01/04/X5	2,000.00			Cash		
Year end 31/03/X6			500.00	1,500.00			
Year end 31/03/X7			375.00	1,125.00			
Year end 31/03/X8							
Year end 31/03/X8							
Computer equipment							
Desktop 132	01/10/X5	1,220.00			Cash		
Year end 31/03/X6			122.00	1,098.00			
Year end 31/03/X7			244.00	854.00			
Year end 31/03/X8							
Laptop 4911	01/01/X6	1,000.00			Cash		
Year end 31/03/X6			50.00	950.00			
Year end 31/03/X7			200.00	750.00			
Year end 31/03/X8							

26 VIVIENNE

You are working on the accounting records of Vivienne for the year ended 31st December 20X7.

- You may ignore VAT.
- An item of computer equipment was part-exchanged on 1 September 20X7.
- The original item was purchased for £4,000 on 12 June 20X3.
- Depreciation is charged at 20% per year on a straight-line basis.
- A full year's depreciation is charged in the year of acquisition but none in the year of disposal.
- A new computer with a list price of £5,000 was acquired through the part-exchange, taking into consideration the part-exchange allowance, Vivienne wrote a cheque for £4,000.

Make entries relating to the disposal by completing the disposals and bank ledger accounts. On each account show clearly the balance to be carried down or transferred to the statement of profit or loss, as appropriate.

Disposals

Picklist: Balance b/d, Balance c/d, Bank, Computer equipment – cost, Computer equipment – accumulated depreciation, Depreciation charges, Disposals, Payables ledger control account, Purchases, Receivables ledger control account, Sales, Statement of profit or loss

Bank

Balance b/d	10,761		

Picklist: Balance b/d, Balance c/d, Bank, Computer equipment – cost, Computer equipment – accumulated depreciation, Depreciation charges, Disposals, Payables ledger control account, Purchases, Receivables ledger control account, Sales, Statement of profit or loss

27 A PARTNERSHIP

You are working on the accounts of a partnership that is registered for VAT.

A new vehicle has been acquired. VAT can be reclaimed on this vehicle. The cost excluding VAT was £7,500; this was paid from the bank. The residual value is expected to be £1,500 excluding VAT. The depreciation policy for vehicles is 25% per annum on a straight-line basis. Depreciation has already been entered into the accounts for the existing vehicles.

Make entries to account for:

(a)   the purchase of the new vehicle

(b)   the depreciation on the new vehicle.

On each account, show clearly the balance carried down or transferred to the statement of profit or loss.

Vehicles at cost

Balance b/d	10,000		

Picklist: Balance b/d, Balance c/d, Bank, Depreciation charges, Disposals, Payables ledger control account, Purchases, Receivables ledger control account, Sales, Statement of profit or loss, Vehicles at cost, Vehicles accumulated depreciation

Vehicles accumulated depreciation

		Balance b/d	3,000

Picklist: Balance b/d, Balance c/d, Bank, Depreciation charges, Disposals, Payables ledger control account, Purchases, Receivables ledger control account, Sales, Statement of profit or loss, Vehicles at cost, Vehicles accumulated depreciation

Depreciation charges

Balance b/d	1,000		

Picklist: Balance b/d, Balance c/d, Bank, Depreciation charges, Disposals, Payables ledger control account, Purchases, Receivables ledger control account, Sales, Statement of profit or loss, Vehicles at cost, Vehicles accumulated depreciation

(c)   **The business needs to develop a policy for authorisation of new vehicles purchases. Choose the ONE most suitable policy.**

New vehicle purchases should be authorised by

	Tick
A partner of the business	
The driver of the vehicle	
A bank signatory	
An accounting technician	

28   SOLE TRADER

You are working on the accounts of a sole trader that is registered for VAT.

A new vehicle has been acquired and VAT can be reclaimed on this vehicle. The cost excluding VAT was £18,000; this was paid from the bank. The residual value is expected to be £6,500 excluding VAT. The depreciation policy for vehicles is 20% per annum on a straight-line basis. Depreciation has already been entered into the accounts for the existing vehicles.

Make entries to account for:

(a)   the purchase of the new vehicle

(b)   the depreciation on the new vehicle.

On each account, show clearly the balance carried down or transferred to the statement of profit or loss.

Vehicles at cost

Balance b/d	26,000		

Picklist: Balance b/d, Balance c/d, Bank, Depreciation charges, Disposals, Payables ledger control account, Purchases, Receivables ledger control account, Sales, Statement of profit or loss, Vehicles at cost, Vehicles accumulated depreciation

Vehicles accumulated depreciation

		Balance b/d	6,500

Picklist: Balance b/d, Balance c/d, Bank, Depreciation charges, Disposals, Payables ledger control account, Purchases, Receivables ledger control account, Sales, Statement of profit or loss, Vehicles at cost, Vehicles accumulated depreciation

29   KATY'S CAKES

- Katy's Cakes is a sole trader business that is registered for VAT. Her year end is 30/04/X0.
- A new industrial sized cake mixer has been acquired. VAT can be reclaimed on this piece of equipment.
- The asset was purchased for cash and cost £8,500 (excluding VAT). This was paid from the bank.
- The depreciation policy for equipment is 10% per annum on a diminishing-balance basis.
- Depreciation on existing equipment has not been accounted for in the year ended 30/04/X0, however there is some depreciation from other categories of asset and this has already been reflected in the depreciation charge account.

Make entries to account for:

(a)   **the purchase of the new equipment**

(b)   **the depreciation on the existing equipment.**

(c)   **the depreciation on the new equipment.**

On each account, show clearly the balance carried down or transferred to the statement of profit or loss.

Equipment at cost

Balance b/d	6,200		

Picklist: Balance b/d, Balance c/d, Bank, Depreciation charges – existing, Depreciation charges – new, Disposals, Payables ledger control account, Purchases, Receivables ledger control account, Sales, Statement of profit or loss

Equipment accumulated depreciation

		Balance b/d	1,900

Picklist: Balance b/d, Balance c/d, Bank, Depreciation charges – existing, Depreciation charges – new, Disposals, Payables ledger control account, Purchases, Receivables ledger control account, Sales, Statement of profit or loss

Depreciation charges

Balance b/d	3,000		

Picklist: Accumulated depreciation – existing, Accumulated depreciation – new, Balance b/d, Balance c/d, Bank, Disposals, Payables ledger control account, Purchases, Receivables ledger control account, Sales, Statement of profit or loss

(d)   **Which ONE of the following statements best describes capital expenditure?**

	✓
The money put in by the owners of the business	
The money spent on the purchase of non-current assets	
The total amount of capital owed to the owner of the business	

30   MILES 2 GO

Miles 2 Go is not registered for VAT and has a year end of 31 December 20X0.

The following is a purchase invoice received by Miles 2 Go:

Invoice # 212532		
To: Miles 2 Go	Graham's Garages	**Date:** 28 November X0
428 Waveney Crescent	32 Cromer Way	
Wellsley	Wellsley	
WY4 GFV	WY12 RTH	
		£
Ford Transit Van	Registration number ES54 DCS	15,000.00
Delivery		250.00
Tax Disc		210.00
Less part-exchange	Registration number FD01 VBA	(3,800.00)
Amount due		11,660.00
Settlement terms: Strictly 60 days		

The following information relates to the vehicle that was part-exchanged:

Registration number	FD01 VBA
Length of ownership	4 years 2 months
Purchase price	£12,000.00

- Vehicles are depreciated at 30% on a diminishing-balance basis.
- Non-current assets are depreciated in the year of acquisition but not in the year of disposal.

You now need to complete the journal to reflect the purchase of the new van and the part-exchange of the old van.

Narrative	Dr	Cr
Totals		

Picklist: Balance b/d, Balance c/d, Bank, Depreciation charges, Disposals, Motor vehicles expenses, Purchases, Sales, Sundry receivables, Sundry payables, Statement of profit or loss, Vehicles accumulated depreciation, Vehicles at cost

31   FLINT FARMS

Flint Farms is not registered for VAT and it has a year end of 30 September 20X0.

The following is a purchase invoice received by Flint Farms:

	Invoice # 493843	
To: Flint Farms	Tony's Tractors	**Date:** 18 August X0
Parkhouse Lane	Somerton Way	
Hinterdon	Hinterdon	
HN5 6LT	HN11 5PZ	
		£
John Deere Tractor	Registration number JT19 7PY	40,000.00
Delivery		800.00
Insurance		2,500.00
Less part-exchange	Registration number NC02 3LS	(8,500.00)
Amount due		34,800.00
Settlement terms: Strictly 60 days		

The following information relates to the vehicle that was part-exchanged:

Registration number	NC02 3LS
Length of ownership	2 years 11 months
Purchase price	£32,000.00

- Vehicles are depreciated at 10% on a diminishing-balance basis.
- Non-current assets are depreciated in the year of acquisition but not in the year of disposal.

(a) **You now need to complete the journal to reflect the purchase of the new van and the part-exchange of the old van.**

Narrative	Dr	Cr
Totals		

(b) **Decide whether the following would be deemed capital or revenue expenditure:**

Rent	
Van	
Installation of air conditioning	
Repairing a window	

Picklist: Balance b/d, Balance c/d, Bank, Depreciation charges, Disposals, Insurance, Motor vehicles expenses, Purchases, Sales, Sundry receivables, Sundry payables, Statement of profit or loss, Vehicle accumulated depreciation, Vehicle at cost

32 LEO LIGHTING

- Leo Lighting is a sole trader business that is registered for VAT at the standard rate of 20%. His year end is 31/12/X4.
- During 20X4, machine 'A' was sold, for total proceeds of £10,000 (cheque received).
- Machine 'A' was acquired on 01/07/X1 at a cost of £20,000 (excluding VAT).
- The depreciation policy for machinery is 10% per annum on a diminishing-balance basis. Non-current assets are depreciated in full in the year of acquisition but not in the year of disposal.

(a) **What is the accumulated depreciation of machine 'A' in the year of disposal?**

(b) **Complete the journal to reflect the disposal of machine 'A'. A picklist of account names has been provided below. You are able to use an account name more than once. More rows than required have been provided below.**

Narrative	Dr	Cr
Totals		

Picklist: Machinery at cost account, Machinery accumulated depreciation account, Disposals account, VAT Control, Bank (accounts can be used more than once)

(c) **What was the profit or loss made on disposal?**

£

33 FRED FARRIER

You are working on the accounting records of Fred Farrier, a sole trader who is registered for VAT at the standard rate of 20%. His accounting year end is 31 December 20X8.

A new piece of equipment has been acquired. VAT can be reclaimed on this piece of equipment.

The cost excluding VAT was £9,250. This was paid from the bank.

The residual value of the piece of equipment is expected to be £1,250 and it is estimated to have a useful life of 5 years.

Equipment is depreciated on a straight-line basis. A full year's depreciation is charged in the year of acquisition. Depreciation on existing equipment has already been accounted for.

(a)   What was the depreciation charge for the year on the new item of equipment?

....

Make entries to account for:

(b)   the purchase of the new item of equipment

(c)   the depreciation charge on the new item of equipment.

On each account, show clearly the balance carried down or transferred to the statement of profit or loss, as appropriate.

Equipment at cost

Balance b/d	38,200		

Picklist: Balance b/d, Balance c/d, Bank, Depreciation charges, Disposals, Purchases, Payables ledger control account, Sales, Receivables ledger control account, Statement of profit or loss

Equipment accumulated depreciation

		Balance b/d	12,200

Picklist: Balance b/d, Balance c/d, Bank, Depreciation charges, Disposals, Payables ledger control account, Purchases, Receivables ledger control account, Sales, Statement of profit or loss

Depreciation charges

Balance b/d	2,300		

Picklist: Accumulated depreciation (equipment), Balance b/d, Balance c/d, Bank, Disposals, Payables ledger control account, Purchases, Receivables ledger control account, Sales, Statement of profit or loss

(d)   A piece of machinery was bought for £9,000, had accumulated depreciation of £4,500 and was disposed of in a part-exchange arrangement. A profit of £1,000 was made on the disposal of the machinery. What was the part-exchange allowance received? Ignore VAT.

....

(e)   Computer equipment was bought for £1,000. Depreciation is charged at 20% using the diminishing-balance method. What is the carrying amount of the computer after three years?

....

RECORD PERIOD END ADJUSTMENTS

34 MULTIPLE CHOICE QUESTIONS

Choose ONE answer from each part.

1 Inventory should be valued at the lower of:

A Cost and net realisable value

B Cost and carrying amount

C Sales and net realisable value

D Sales and carrying amount

2 Which accounting term is defined as accounting for an expense that has been incurred but the cash has not yet been paid?

A A prepayment

B An accrual

C Depreciation

D Deferred income

3 Which statement provides the most appropriate explanation of irrecoverable debts?

A Amounts that are owed by customers that might not be received

B Amounts that are owed by customers that have been received

C Amounts that are owed by customers that will not be received

4 Which ONE of the statements below explains the classification of a prepayment in the financial statements?

A An expense in the statement of profit or loss

B An asset in the statement of financial position

C Income in the statement of profit or loss

D A liability in the statement of financial position

5 Arty Partners has the following items of inventory at 31 December 20X9.

Component	Number held	Unit cost	Unit selling price
		£	£
A	100	3.00	3.60
B	150	2.50	2.70
C	20	4.50	4.20

What is the total value of inventory in the statement of financial position as at 31 December 20X9?

A £855

B £849

C £759

D £765

6   **Rent paid on 1 October 20X2 for the year to 30 September 20X3 was £1,200 and rent paid on 1 October 20X3 for the year to 30 September 20X4 was £1,600. What is the rent payable, as shown in the statement of profit or loss for the year ended 31 December 20X3?**

    A   £1,200

    B   £1,600

    C   £1,300

    D   £1,500

7   A summary of the transactions of R Sandstone, who is VAT registered, showed the following for the month of May 20X5.

Outputs £80,000 (excluding VAT)

Inputs £64,200 (including VAT)

At the beginning of the period R Sandstone owed £4,500 to HM Revenue and Customs, and during the period R Sandstone paid £3,600 to HM Revenue and Customs.

At the end of the period, how much is owing to HM Revenue and Customs?

    A   £2,800

    B   £4,400

    C   £6,200

    D   £13,400

8   The balance on the payables ledger control account was £3,446. It was then discovered that the total from the cash book payments during the period had been posted as £14,576 instead of £14,756. It was also discovered that a contra with the receivables ledger control account of £392 had not been posted at all.

What is the correct balance carried down on the payables ledger control account?

    A   £2,874

    B   £3,234

    C   £3,658

    D   £4,018

9   **Memorandum (subsidiary) receivables ledger accounts are kept to**

    A   Summarise the total sales for the business

    B   Show how much customers owe in total

    C   Show how much each individual customer owes

    D   Enable the production of individual supplier statements

10 **Which of the following are limitations of the trial balance?**

1 It does not include all final figures to be included in the financial statements.

2 It does not identify all errors of commission.

3 It does not identify in which accounts errors have been made.

A 1 and 2 only

B 2 and 3 only

C 1, 2 and 3

D 1 and 3 only

35 DAYTIME

You are working on the accounting records of a business, Daytime, for the year ended 31 March 20X8. In this task you may ignore VAT.

You have the following information:

The balance on the commission receivable account at the beginning of the financial year is £3,200. This represents an accrual for commission receivable at the end of the year on 31 March 20X7. The bank summary for the year shows receipts for commission receivable of £22,800. The commission receivable account has been correctly adjusted for £2,800 commission for the quarter ended 31 March 20X8. This was received into the bank and entered into our accounting records on 21 April 20X8. Double entry is done in the general ledger.

(a) **Complete the following statements:**

On 01/04/X7, the commission receivable account shows a _____ (debit/credit) balance of £_____. On 31/03/X8 the commission receivable account shows an adjustment for_____ (accrued income/prepaid income/accrued expenses/prepaid expenses) of £_____.

(b) **Calculate the commission receivable for the year ended 31 March 20X8:**

£_____.

(c) The bank summary for the year shows payments for telephone expenses of £1,896.

Update the telephone expense account for this, showing clearly the amount transferred to the statement of profit or loss.

Telephone expenses

Reversal of prepaid expenses	125		

(d)   You now find a bill related to telephone expenses that has not been included in the accounting records. The bill totals £330 and relates to the three month period ending 31 May 20X8. Taking into account this information, complete the following statements, please note you are not required to go back and amend your answer to part (c).

The amount to be transferred to the statement of profit or loss for telephone expenses will be £_____ _____ (greater/less) than the figure in (c).

Telephone expenses will show as a _____ (debit/credit) balance in the statement of profit or loss account in the general ledger.

36   NIGHTIME

You are working on the accounting records of a business, Nightime, for the year ended 31 December 20X8. In this task you may ignore VAT.

You have the following information:

The balance on the rental income account at the beginning of the financial year is £1,800. This represents prepaid rental income at the end of the year on 31 December 20X7. The bank summary for the year shows receipts for rent of £18,000. As part of the £18,000 received during the year, £2,000 was received that relates to a rental income for the next financial year. The rental income has been correctly adjusted for this amount. Double entry is done in the general ledger.

(a)   **Complete the following statements:**

On 01/01/X8, the rental income account shows a _____ (debit/credit) balance of £_____. On 31/12/X8 the rental income account shows an adjustment for_____ (accrued income/prepaid income/accrued expenses/prepaid expenses) of £_____.

(b)   **Calculate the rental income for the year ended 31 December 20X8: £_____**

(c)   **The bank summary for the year shows payments for office expenses of £2,600.**

Update the office expenses account for this, showing clearly the amount transferred to the statement of profit or loss.

Office expenses

		Reversal of accrued expenses	120

(d) You now find a bill related for secretarial services that has not been included in the accounting records. The bill totals £1,200 and relates to the three month period ending 31 January 20X9. Taking into account this information, complete the following statements (please note you are not required to go back and amend your answer to part (c).

The amount to be transferred to the statement of profit or loss for office expenses will be £_____ _____ (greater/less) than the figure in (c).

Office expenses will show as a _____ (debit/credit) balance in the statement of profit or loss in the general ledger.

37 COLETTE

You are working on the accounting records of Colette, a sole trader with a financial year end of 31 December 20X8. Ignore VAT.

You are provided with the following information relating to general expenses.

- The balance on the general expenses account as at the beginning of the financial year was £1,000, this represents an amount incurred in the prior year.

- The cashbook for the year shows general expenses of £8,500 have been paid during 20X8.

- General expenses have been adjusted for an expense of £750 which was paid for in December 20X8 but which relates to January 20X9.

(a) Show how the general expenses account in the general ledger looked at the beginning of the financial year. You should insert ONE date, ONE description and ONE amount in the correct position in the ledger account.

General expenses

Date	Description	Dr	Date	Description	Cr

Date picklist: 31/12/20X7, 1/1/20X8, 31/12/20X8

Description picklist: Accrued expenses reversal, Prepaid expenses reversal

Amount picklist: £750, £1,000

(b) Complete the following statement.

On the 31st December 20X8 the general ledger account for general expenses shows a [   ] (debit/credit) entry for [   ] (accrued expenses/prepaid expenses) carried down of £[   ].

(c) Calculate the general expenses balance for the year ended 31 December 20X8.

£[   ].

38 MAIKI

You are working on the accounting records of Maiki, a sole trader with a financial year end of 31 March 20X7. Ignore VAT.

You are provided with the following information relating to sundry expenses.

- The balance on the sundry expenses account at the beginning of the financial year was £1,500 which represents an amount paid in advance.
- The cashbook for the year shows sundry expenses of £11,500 have been paid.
- Sundry expenses have been adjusted for an expense of £500 which was paid for in April 20X7 but which relates to March 20X7.

(a) **Show how the sundry expenses account in the general ledger looked at the beginning of the financial year. You should insert ONE date, ONE description and ONE amount in the correct position in the ledger account.**

Sundry expenses

Date	Description	Dr	Date	Description	Cr

Date picklist: 31/3/20X6, 1/4/20X6, 31/3/20X7

Description picklist: Accrued expenses reversal, Prepaid expenses reversal

Amount picklist: £500, £1,500

(b) **Complete the following statement.**

On the 31st March 20X7 the general ledger account for sundry expenses shows a [　　] (debit/credit) entry for [　　　　　　　　　　　] (accrued expenses/prepaid expenses) carried down of £[　　　　].

(c) **Calculate the sundry expenses balance for the year ended 31 March 20X7.**

£[　　　　].

39 RENTAL EXPENSES

The policy of the business for accruals and prepayments is as follows:

An entry is made into the income or expense account and an opposite entry into the relevant asset or liability account. In the following period the entry is reversed.

You are looking at rental expenses for the year ended 31 March 20X7.

The cash book for the year shows payments for rent of £10,550.

This includes payments for 2 properties as follows:

Rental for the period:

Property A: 1 January to 31 December 20X7 £1,500

Property B: 1 April 20X7 to 31 March 20X8 £2,900

(a) **Calculate the value of the adjustment required for rental expenses as at 31 March 20X7.**

£[　　　　].

(b) **Update the rental expenses account. You must show:**

- the cash book figure
- the year-end adjustment
- the transfer to the statement or profit or loss for the year.

Rental expenses

Prepaid expenses (reversal)	1,800		

Picklist: Accrued expenses, Bank, Prepaid expenses, Rent, Statement of profit or loss

40 BANK RECONCILIATION I

The bank statement has been compared with the cash book and the following differences identified:

1 Bank interest paid of £82 was not entered in the cash book.

2 A cheque paid for £450 has been incorrectly entered in the cash book as £540.

3 Cheques totalling £1,980 paid into the bank at the end of the month are not showing on the bank statement.

4 A BACS receipt of £1,750 from a customer has not been entered in the cash book.

The balance showing on the bank statement is a credit of £5,250 and the balance in the cash book is a debit of £5,472.

Use the following table to show the THREE adjustments you need to make to the cash book.

Adjustment	Amount £	Debit/Credit

41 BANK RECONCILIATION II

The bank statement has been compared with the cash book and the following differences identified:

1 Cheques totalling £1,629 paid into the bank at the end of the month are not showing on the bank statement.

2 Bank interest paid of £106 was not entered in the cash book.

3 A cheque for £350 written on 2 June has been incorrectly entered in the cash book at 2 May.

4   A receipt from a customer of £1,645 has cleared the bank but has not been entered in the cash book.

The balance showing on the bank statement at 31 May is a credit of £363 and the balance in the cash book is a debit of £103.

Use the following table to show the THREE adjustments you need to make to the cash book.

Adjustment	Amount £	Debit/Credit

42   BANK RECONCILIATION III

Which three of the following differences between a company's cashbook balance and its bank statement balance as at 30 November 20X9 would feature in the bank reconciliation statement?

1   Cheques recorded and sent to suppliers before 30 November 20X9 but not yet presented for payment.

2   Omission by the bank of a lodgement made by the company on 26 November 20X9.

3   Bank charges.

4   Cheques paid in before 30 November 20X9 but not credited by the bank until 3 December 20X9.

5   A customer's cheque recorded and paid in before 30 November 20X9 but dishonoured by the bank.

A   1, 2 and 3

B   1, 3 and 5

C   1, 2 and 4

D   3, 4 and 5

43   PAYABLES LEDGER CONTROL ACCOUNT I

You are working on the final accounts of a business.

You have the following information:

(a)   A payment of £4,185 to a supplier has been credited to the supplier's account in the payables ledger.

(b)   A supplier with a balance of £2,170 has been listed as £2,710.

(c)   A credit purchase of £750 (including VAT) has not been included in the relevant supplier's account in the payables ledger.

(d)   A casting error has been made and one of the supplier accounts has been undercast by £462.

(e)   A supplier account with a balance of £1,902 has been omitted from the list.

(f)   Purchase returns totalling £540 has been entered twice in error.

You now need to make the appropriate adjustments in the table below. For each adjustment clearly state the amount and whether the item should be added or subtracted from the list of balances.

	Add/Subtract	£
Total from list of balances		52,750
Adjustment for (a)		
Adjustment for (b)		
Adjustment for (c)		
Adjustment for (d)		
Adjustment for (e)		
Adjustment for (f)		
Revised total to agree with PLCA		47,494

44   PAYABLES LEDGER CONTROL ACCOUNT II

You are working on the final accounts of a business

You have the following information:

(a)   A payment of £1,277 to a supplier has been debited to the supplier's account in the payables ledger as £1,722.

(b)   A supplier with a debit balance of £2,170 has been listed as a credit balance.

(c)   A credit purchase return of £1,000 (net of VAT at 20%) has not been included in the relevant supplier's account in the payables ledger.

(d)   A casting error has been made and one of the supplier accounts has been overcast by £132.

(e)   A supplier account with a balance of £2,100 has been omitted from the list.

(f)   A credit purchase has been entered into the individual account net of VAT at 20%. The net amount is £600.

You now need to make the appropriate adjustments in the table below. For each adjustment clearly state the amount and whether the item should be added or subtracted from the list of balances.

	Add/Subtract	£
Total from list of balances		132,589
Adjustment for (a)		
Adjustment for (b)		
Adjustment for (c)		
Adjustment for (d)		
Adjustment for (e)		
Adjustment for (f)		
Revised total to agree with PLCA		129,582

45 RECEIVABLES LEDGER CONTROL ACCOUNT I

You are working on the final accounts of a business.

You have the following information:

(a) A casting error has been made and one of the customer accounts has been overcast by £73.

(b) Sales returns totalling £280 has been entered twice in error.

(c) A receipt of £2,771 from a customer has been debited to the customer's account in the receivables ledger.

(d) A credit sale of £3,090 (including VAT) has not been included in the relevant customer's account in the receivables ledger.

(e) A customer account with a balance of £935 has been omitted from the list.

(f) A customer with a balance of £4,725 has been listed as £4,275.

You now need to make the appropriate adjustments in the table below. For each adjustment clearly state the amount and whether the item should be added or subtracted from the list of balances.

	Add/Subtract	£
Total from list of balances		31,820
Adjustment for (a)		
Adjustment for (b)		
Adjustment for (c)		
Adjustment for (d)		
Adjustment for (e)		
Adjustment for (f)		
Revised total to agree with RLCA		30,960

46   RECEIVABLES LEDGER CONTROL ACCOUNT II

You are working on the final accounts of a business.

You have the following information:

(a)   A casting error has been made and one of the customer accounts has been undercast by £65.

(b)   Sales returns totalling £280 have not been entered in a customer's individual ledger.

(c)   A receipt of £1,300 from a customer has been credited to the customer's account in the receivables ledger as 130.

(d)   A credit sale of £3,000 (excluding VAT at 20%) has not been included in the relevant customer's account in the receivables ledger.

(e)   A customer account with a balance of £99 has been duplicated in the list of balances.

(f)   A customer with a credit balance of £50 has been listed as a debit balance of £50.

You now need to make the appropriate adjustments in the table below. For each adjustment clearly state the amount and whether the item should be added or subtracted from the list of balances. If no adjustment is required enter '0' into the amount column.

	Add/Subtract	£
Total from list of balances		31,100
Adjustment for (a)		
Adjustment for (b)		
Adjustment for (c)		
Adjustment for (d)		
Adjustment for (e)		
Adjustment for (f)		
Revised total to agree with RLCA		33,116

47   BRODIE

You are working on the accounting records of Brodie. A trial balance has been drawn up. You need to make some corrections and adjustments for the year ended 31 March 20X9. You may ignore VAT in this task.

Record the journal entries needed in the general ledger to deal with the items below.

You should remove any incorrect entries where appropriate and post the correct entries.

You do not need to give any narratives.

(a)   The following adjustment for closing inventory has already been made in the accounts:

Dr Closing inventory (SFP) £10,000

Cr Closing inventory (SPL) £10,000

This adjustment was made without the knowledge that closing inventory of £2,000 can only be sold for 90% of the original cost.

You are required to remove the incorrect entry from the accounts and enter the revised closing inventory into the accounts.

Journal

	Dr £	Cr £

(b) Computer equipment is depreciated on a diminishing-balance basis at a rate of 10% per annum. As at 1 April 20X8 the balances of computer equipment at cost and the associated accumulated depreciation were £127,620 and £47,100 respectively. Enter the adjustment for the depreciation charge for the year ended 31 March 20X9. No additions or disposals were made during the year.

Journal

	Dr £	Cr £

(c) Following on from the information in part (b) -

What is the revised carrying amount of Computer Equipment as at 31 March 20X9?

....

(d) Brodie trades regularly with Carrie & Co. A contra entry for the value of £21,456 needs to be entered into the accounts for the year ended 31 March 20X9.

Journal

	Dr £	Cr £

PRODUCE AND EXTEND THE TRIAL BALANCE

48 MULTIPLE CHOICE QUESTIONS

Choose ONE answer from each part.

1 **It is important to produce a trial balance prior to preparing the financial statements because:**

A it confirms the accuracy of the ledger accounts

B it provides all the figures necessary to prepare the financial statements

C it shows that the ledger accounts contain debit and credit entries of an equal value

D it enables the accountant to calculate any adjustments required

2 **The debit side of a trial balance totals £50 more than the credit side. This could be due to:**

A a purchase of goods for £50 being omitted from the payables account

B a sale of goods for £50 being omitted from the receivables account

C an invoice of £25 for electricity being credited to the electricity account

D a receipt for £50 from a receivable being omitted from the cash book

3 **A trial balance guarantees there are no errors in the accounting records.**

A True

B False

4 **When extending the trial balance, if the debit column of the statement of profit or loss is £125,000 and the credit column is £137,000, what entry would be required?**

A None

B Dr Statement of profit or loss £12,000/Cr statement of financial position £12,000

C Dr Statement of profit or loss £12,000

D Dr Statement of financial position £12,000/Cr statement of profit or loss £12,000

5 **Referring back to question 4, is this a profit or a loss?**

A Profit

B Loss

49 EXPENSES LEDGER ACCOUNTS I

You are given the following information (ignore VAT):

Balances as at:	1 April 20X0 £
Accrual for administration expenses	790
Prepayment for selling expenses	475

The bank summary for the year shows payments for administration expenses of £7,190. Included in this figure is £2,700 for the quarter ended 31 May 20X1.

(a) **Prepare the administration expenses account for the year ended 31 March 20X1 and close it off by showing the transfer to the statement of profit or loss.**

Administration expenses

The bank summary for the year shows payments for selling expenses of £7,900. In April 20X1, £900 was paid for selling expenses incurred in March 20X1.

(b)   Prepare the selling expenses account for the year ended 31 March 20X1 and close it off by showing the transfer to the statement of profit or loss.

Selling expenses

You have the following extract of balances from the general ledger.

(c)   Using your answers to (a) and (b), and the figures given below, enter amounts in the appropriate column for the accounts shown.

Extract from trial balance as at 31 March 20X1.

Account	£	Dr £	Cr £
Accruals			
Capital	6,000		
Wages and salaries	850		
Selling expenses			
Drawings	11,000		
Administration expenses			
Interest received	70		
Machinery at cost	5,600		
Machinery accumulated depreciation	4,200		
Prepayments			

50   EXPENSES LEDGER ACCOUNTS II

You are given the following information (ignore VAT):

Balances as at:	1 April 20X5 £
Accrual for electricity expenses	2,815
Prepayment for rental expenses	6,250

The bank summary for the year shows payments for electricity expenses of £10,539. Included in this figure is £2,358 for the quarter ended 31 May 20X6.

(a)   **Prepare the electricity expenses account for the year ended 31 March 20X6 and close it off by showing the transfer to the statement of profit or loss.**

Electricity expenses

The bank summary for the year shows payments for rental expenses of £62,500. In April 20X6, £6,250 was paid late relating to March 20X6 rent.

(b)   **Prepare the rental expenses account for the year ended 31 March 20X6 and close it off by showing the transfer to the statement of profit or loss.**

Rental expenses

You have the following extract of balances from the general ledger.

(c)   **Using your answers to (a) and (b), and the figures given below, enter amounts in the appropriate column for the accounts shown.**

Extract from trial balance as at 31 March 20X6.

Account	£	Dr £	Cr £
Accruals			
Accumulated depreciation – Office equipment	17,921		
Depreciation charge	3,805		
Drawings	22,400		
Electricity			
Interest received	129		
Office equipment – cost	42,784		
Rental			
Stationery	2,800		
Prepayments			

51 EXPENSES LEDGER ACCOUNTS III

You have the following information (ignore VAT):

Balances as at:	1 Jan 20X8
	£
Accrual for telephone expenses	4,375
Prepayment for rates expenses	5,000

The bank summary for the year shows payments for telephone expenses of £12,645. Included in this figure is £4,278 for the quarter ended 31 Jan 20X9.

(a) **Prepare the telephone expenses account for the year ended 31 December 20X8 and close it off by showing the transfer to the statement of profit or loss.**

Telephone expenses

The bank summary for the year shows payments for rates expenses of £82,750. In January 20X9, £8,250 was paid late relating to December 20X8 rates.

(b) **Prepare the rates expenses account for the year ended 31 December 20X8 and close it off by showing the transfer to the statement of profit or loss.**

Rates expenses

You have the following extract of balances from the general ledger.

(c)   Using your answers to (a) and (b), and the figures given below, enter amounts in the appropriate column for the accounts shown.

Extract from trial balance as at 31 December 20X8

Account	£	Dr £	Cr £
Accruals			
Accumulated depreciation – Machinery	15,437		
Bank charges	2,897		
Capital	27,000		
Discounts allowed	520		
Light and heat	4,000		
Machinery – cost	41,697		
Prepayments			
Rates			
Telephone			

52   RENT

You are given the following information (ignore VAT):

(a)   Rent paid on 1 January 20X6 for the year to 31 December 20X6 was £1,800 and rent paid on 1 January 20X7 for the year to 31 December 20X7 was £2,400. The rent expense as shown in the statement of profit or loss for the year ended 30 September 20X7 and the prepayment at that date, would be:

Statement of profit or loss: £..................

Prepayment: £..................

(b)   The electricity account for the year ended 30 September 20X7 was as follows:

Opening balance for electricity accrued at 1 October 20X6	£200
Payments made during the year:	
1 December for 3 months to 30 November 20X6	£600
1 March 20X7 for 3 months to 28 February 20X7	£800
1 June 20X7 for 3 months to 31 May 20X7	£750
1 September 20X7 for 3 months to 31 August 20X7	£525

What is the appropriate entry for electricity?

Accrued at 30 September 20X7	Charge to the statement of profit or loss year ended 30 September 20X7
£	£

(c) Using your answers to (a) and (b), and the figures given below, enter amounts in the appropriate column for the accounts shown.

Extract from trial balance as at 30 September 20X7.

Account	£	Dr £	Cr £
Accruals			
Capital	100,000		
Wages and salaries	25,000		
Rental expense			
Drawings	5,000		
Electricity expense			
Interest paid	950		
Computer equipment at cost	4,575		
Computer equipment accumulated depreciation	1,550		
Prepayments			

53 ANDREAS

You are working on the accounting records of Andreas with a year end of 30 June 20X6. You have five extracts from the ledger accounts for the year ended 30 June 20X6. You need to start preparing the trial balance as at 30 June 20X6.

Discounts received

Date	Description	Dr (£)	Date	Description	Cr (£)
			30/6/X6	Bal b/f	300

Irrecoverable debts expense

Date	Description	Dr (£)	Date	Description	Cr (£)
30/6/X6	Bal b/f	1,987			

Rental income

Date	Description	Dr (£)	Date	Description	Cr (£)
			30/6/X6	Bal b/f	3,000

The rental income balance has already been adjusted for prepaid income of £500

Electricity

Date	Description	Dr (£)	Date	Description	Cr (£)
30/6/X6	Bal b/f	450			

Electricity expense needs to be adjusted for a prepaid expense of £100

Bank

Date	Description	Dr (£)	Date	Description	Cr (£)
30/6/X6	Bal b/f	11,000			

There were no other accruals or prepayments of income or expense other than those detailed above.

(a) **Using all the information given above and the balances given in the table below, enter the amounts into the appropriate trial balance columns for the accounts shown.**

Extract from trial balance as at 30 June 20X6.

Account	£	Dr £	Cr £
Bank			
Capital	24,198		
Discounts received			
Electricity			
Fixtures & fittings at cost	11,000		
Fixtures & fittings accumulated depreciation	2,400		
Irrecoverable debt expense			
Misc. expense	2,600		
Prepaid expense			
Prepaid income			
Rental income			
Stationery	55		

You are now ready to prepare the reconciliation of the receivables ledger control account (receivables control account) to the receivables ledger.

The total of the balance on the receivables ledger control account is £9,500 compared to the total of the balances on the receivables ledger being £9,507. On investigation the following errors have been discovered:

1   A customer account with a debit balance of £157 was duplicated in error.

2   A contra entry for £100 was not made in the memorandum ledger or the control account in the general ledger.

3   A sales return of £350 from a customer was not posted in the receivables ledger control account in the general ledger.

4   The discounts allowed total of £200 was entered twice into the receivables ledger control account.

(b) Use the following table to show the TWO adjustments required to the listing of the Receivables ledger. For the 'Add' and 'Deduct' columns, tick as appropriate.

Adjustment number	Amount (£)	Add	Deduct

(c) Use the following table to show the THREE adjustments required to the RECEIVABLES LEDGER CONTROL account in the GENERAL ledger. For the 'Debit' and 'Credit' columns, tick as appropriate.

Adjustment number	Amount (£)	Debit	Credit

54 KYLE

You are working on the accounting records of Kyle with a year end of 31 December. You have five extracts from the ledger accounts for the year ended 31 December 20X6. You need to start preparing the trial balance as at 31 December 20X6.

Allowance for doubtful receivables adjustment

Date	Description	Dr (£)	Date	Description	Cr (£)
			31/12/X6	Bal b/f	160

Discount allowed

Date	Description	Dr (£)	Date	Description	Cr (£)
31/12/X6	Bal b/f	575			

General expenses

Date	Description	Dr (£)	Date	Description	Cr (£)
31/12/X6	Bal b/f	2,250			

The general expenses balance needs to be adjusted for a closing accrual of £250.

Commission received

Date	Description	Dr (£)	Date	Description	Cr (£)
			31/12/X6	Bal b/f	450

Commission received needs adjusting for income that was received by cheque of £200

Drawings

Date	Description	Dr (£)	Date	Description	Cr (£)
31/12/X6	Bal b/f	1,000			

There were no other accruals other than the accrual for general expenses detailed above.

(a) **Using all the information given above and the balances given in the table below, enter the amounts into the appropriate trial balance columns for the accounts shown.**

Extract from trial balance as at 31 December 20X6.

Account	£	Dr £	Cr £
Accruals			
Capital	25,000		
Wages and salaries	2,400		
Allowance for doubtful receivables adjustment			
Receivables	11,000		
Drawings			
Entertainment expense	70		
Computer equipment at cost	2,600		
Computer equipment accumulated depreciation	1,200		
Commission received			
General expenses			
Discount allowed			

You are now ready to prepare the reconciliation of the payables ledger control account to the payables ledger.

The total of the balance on the payables ledger control account is £11,500 compared to the total of the balances on the payables ledger being £12,150. On investigation the following errors have been discovered:

1   A supplier account with a credit balance of £450 was duplicated in error.

2   A contra entry for £100 was made in the memorandum ledger but was not entered into the control account in the general ledger.

3   A cash payment of £100 to a supplier was omitted from a supplier's individual account but was correctly posted in the general ledger.

4   The discounts received total of £200 was entered twice into the payables ledger control account.

(b) Use the following table to show the TWO adjustments required to the listing of the Payables ledger. For the 'Add' and 'Deduct' columns, tick as appropriate.

Adjustment number	Amount (£)	Add	Deduct

(c) Use the following table to show the TWO adjustments required to the PAYABLES LEDGER CONTROL account in the GENERAL ledger. For the 'Debit' and 'Credit' columns, tick as appropriate.

Adjustment number	Amount (£)	Debit	Credit

55 JACKSONS

You are working on the final accounts of Jacksons, a business with a year end of 31 May. A trial balance has been drawn up and a suspense account opened with a credit balance of £1,200. You need to make some corrections and adjustments for the year ended 31 May 20X1.

(a) Record the adjustments needed on the extract from the extended trial balance to deal with the items below. (You will not need to enter adjustments on every line)

   (i) Entries need to be made for an irrecoverable debt of £220.

   (ii) A loan repayment of £1,600 has been made. The correct entry was made to the loan account but no other entries were made.

   (iii) No entries have been made for closing inventory for the year-end 31 May 20X1. Closing inventory has been valued at cost at £18,500. Included in this figure are some items costing £2,500 that will be sold for £1,700.

   (iv) The figures from the columns of the sales day book for 23 May have been totalled correctly as follows:

Sales column	£2,000
VAT column	£400
Total column	£2,400

The amounts have been posted as follows:

Cr Sales	£2,000
Cr VAT	£400
Dr Receivables ledger control account	£2,000

Extract from extended trial balance

	Ledger balances		Adjustments	
	Dr £	Cr £	Dr £	Cr £
Allowance for doubtful receivables		365		
Bank	4,300			
Closing inventory – statement of financial position				
Closing inventory – Statement of profit or loss				
Depreciation charge				
Irrecoverable debts				
Loan		4,000		
Loan interest	240			
Plant and machinery – accumulated depreciation		22,000		
Revenue		210,000		
Receivables ledger control account	24,500			
Suspense		1,200		
VAT		5,600		

(b) **The ledgers are ready to be closed off for the year ended 31 May 20X1. Show the correct entries to close off the loan interest account and include an appropriate narrative.**

Account	Debit/Credit

56   PERCY

You are working on the final accounts of your friend Percy's business with a year-end of 31 December. A trial balance has been drawn up and a suspense account opened with a debit balance of £9,630. You need to make some corrections and adjustments for the year ended 31 December 20X1.

Record the journal entries needed in the general ledger to deal with the items below. You do not need to give narrative.

You should remove any incorrect entries, where appropriate, and post the correct entries.

(a)   Two customers have been identified as having problems paying. Borrett Ltd owes £500 and hasn't made any payments for 3 months. Abbott & Co owes £715 and Percy has received notice of their liquidation.

Journal

	Dr £	Cr £

(b)   A payment of £880 for repairs to the business van has been made from the bank. The correct entry was made to the bank account but no other entries were made.

Journal

	Dr £	Cr £

(c)   No entries have been made for closing inventory for the year end 31 December 20X1. Closing inventory has been valued at cost at £33,821. Included in this figure are some items costing £5,211 that will be sold for £3,000.

Journal

	Dr £	Cr £

(d)   The figures from the columns of the purchases day book for 23 December have been totalled correctly as follows:

Purchases column	£25,000
VAT column	£4,375
Total column	£29,375

The amounts have been posted as follows:

Dr Purchases	£25,000
Cr VAT	£4,375
Cr Payables ledger control account	£29,375

Journal

	Dr £	Cr £

57 MERCURY DELIVERIES

Mercury Deliveries has a year end of 31 May. A trial balance has been drawn up and a suspense account opened with a credit balance of £12,525. You need to make some corrections and adjustments for the year ended 31 May 20X1.

Record the journal entries needed in the general ledger to deal with the items below. You do not need to give narrative.

You should remove any incorrect entries, where appropriate, and post the correct entries.

(a) **A payment of £275 for printer cartridges and paper has been made from the bank. The correct entry was made to the bank, but no other entries were made.**

Journal

	Dr £	Cr £

(b) **No entries have been made for closing inventory, which has been valued at £34,962. After the year end, items which had originally been purchased for £2,741, were sold for £3,600.**

Journal

	Dr £	Cr £

(c) Notice has been received of the liquidation of Kat Ltd. The receivables ledger account shows a balance of £210.

Journal

	Dr £	Cr £

(d) The figures from the columns of the sales day book for 15 April have been totalled correctly as follows:

Sales column	£32,000
VAT column	£6,400
Total column	£38,400

The amounts have been posted as follows:

Dr Receivables ledger control account	£38,400
Dr VAT	£6,400
Cr Revenue	£32,000

Journal

	Dr £	Cr £

58   EVANS AND CO

You are employed by Evans and Co, a bicycle manufacturer as their bookkeeper and they have asked you to create a trial balance. Below are the balances extracted from the main ledger at 31 May 20X0.

(a)   **Enter the balances into the columns of the trial balance provided below. Total the two columns and enter an appropriate suspense account balance to ensure that the two totals agree.**

	£	Debit	Credit
Capital	50,000		50,000
Purchases	83,468	83,468	
Revenue	159,407		159,407
Purchase returns	2,693		2,693
Sales returns	3,090	3,090	
RLCA	25,642	25,642	
PLCA	31,007		31,007
Drawings	25,500	25,500	
Machinery – Cost	45,900		
Machinery – Accumulated depreciation	15,925		
Rent and rates	15,600		
Light and heat	2,466		
Motor expenses	2,603		
Loan	12,500		
Interest paid	1,250		
Discounts received	400		
Irrecoverable debts	1,300		
Allowances for doubtful receivables	2,572		
Salaries	77,921		
Bank overdraft	3,876		
Suspense			
Totals			

(b)   You are told of the following errors:

(i)   Drawings of £1,000 have been debited to the salaries account.

(ii)   The net column of the PDB has been overcast by £280.

(iii)   The VAT column of the SDB has been undercast by £70.

(iv)   An amount of £3,175 paid for rent and rates has been debited to both the rent and rates account and the bank account.

(v)   An accrual for electricity at the year end of £340 has been correctly credited to the accruals account but no other entry has been made.

Prepare the entries to correct these errors using the blank journal below. Dates and narratives are not required.

		Dr £	Cr £
(i)			
(ii)			
(iii)			
(iv)			
(v)			

59   RACHEL EDMUNDSON

You are employed by Rachel Edmundson who is a florist. You are her bookkeeper and she has asked you to create a trial balance. Below are the balances extracted from the main ledger at 30 April 20X2.

(a)   **Enter the balances into the columns of the trial balance provided below. Total the two columns and enter an appropriate suspense account balance to ensure that the two totals agree.**

	£	Debit	Credit
Accruals	4,820		
Prepayments	2,945		
Motor expenses	572		
Admin expenses	481		
Light and Heat	1,073		
Revenue	48,729		
Purchases	26,209		
RLCA	5,407		
PLCA	3,090		
Rent	45		
Purchase returns	306		
Discounts allowed	567		
Capital	10,000		
Loan	15,000		
Interest paid	750		
Drawings	4,770		
Motor vehicles – cost	19,000		
Motor vehicle – accumulated depreciation	2,043		
VAT control owing	2,995		
Wages	20,000		
Suspense account			
Totals			

(b) Since the trial balance has been produced you have noticed a number of errors which are as follows:

(i) Rachel put £5,000 into the business after receiving a large cheque as a Christmas present from her Gran. This has been put through the bank account but no other entries have been made.

(ii) The Gross column of the SDB has been overcast by £385.

(iii) The VAT column of the PDB has been undercast by £193.

(iv) An amount of £4,500 paid for rent has been credited to both the rent account and the bank account.

(v) An accrual for electricity at the year end of £1,356 has been correctly credited to the accruals account but no other entry has been made.

Prepare the entries to correct these errors using the blank journal below. Dates and narratives are not required.

		Dr £	Cr
(i)			
(ii)			
(iii)			
(iv)			
(v)			

60 BUSTER

You are working on the accounting records of Buster. A trial balance has been drawn up and a suspense account opened. You need to make some corrections and adjustments for the year ended 31 December 20X8. You may ignore VAT in this task.

Record the journal entries needed in the general ledger to deal with the items below.

You should remove any incorrect entries where appropriate and post the correct entries.

You do not need to give any narratives.

(a) Motor expenses of £4,500 have been posted to the Motor Vehicles at Cost account in error. The other side of the entry is correct.

Journal

	Dr £	Cr £

(b) Office sundries costing £16 were paid for by cash. Only the entry to the cash account was made.

Journal

	Dr £	Cr £

(c) No entries have been made for closing inventory as at 31 December 20X8. It has been valued at a selling price of £227,184. The sales price has had 20% added onto its original cost.

Journal

	Dr £	Cr £

(d) Discounts allowed of £1,270 have been posted as £1,720 on both sides of the entry.

Journal

	Dr £	Cr £

61   PAYROLL COSTS

Selecting from the pick lists available, show the correct accounting entries required at each stage of the process when accounting for payroll costs.

Step 1 – Account for the total wages expense to the employer.

Debit	Wages expense/Wages and salaries control/HMRC payable/Bank/Pension payable
Credit	Wages expense/Wages and salaries control/HMRC payable/Bank/Pension payable

Step 2 – Account for the payment of net pay to the employees.

Debit	Wages expense/Wages and salaries control/HMRC payable/Bank/Pension payable
Credit	Wages expense/Wages and salaries control/HMRC payable/Bank/Pension payable

Step 3 – Account for the PAYE, employer's NIC and employees' NIC payable to HM Revenue and Customs.

Debit	Wages expense/Wages and salaries control/HMRC payable/Bank/Pension payable
Credit	Wages expense/Wages and salaries control/HMRC payable/Bank/Pension payable

Step 4 – Account for the employees' pension contributions due to the pension fund.

Debit	Wages expense/Wages and salaries control/HMRC payable/Bank/Pension payable
Credit	Wages expense/Wages and salaries control/HMRC payable/Bank/Pension payable

62   CARTERS

You have the following extended trial balance. The adjustments have already been correctly entered. You now need to extend the figures into the statement of profit or loss and statement of financial position columns. Make the columns balance by entering figures and a label in the correct places.

Extended trial balance

	Ledger account	Ledger balances Dr £	Cr £	Adjustments Dr £	Cr £	Statement of profit or loss Dr £	Cr £	Statement of financial position Dr £	Cr £
F	Allowance for doubtful receivables		1,300	600					700
P+L	Allowance for doubtful receivables adjustment				600	600			
F	Bank	28,380			500			27,880	
F	Capital		4,530						4,530
	Closing inventory			40,000	40,000		40,000	40,000	
P+L	Depreciation charge			20,500		20,500			
P+L	Office expenses	69,550			500	69,050			
P+L	Opening inventory	26,000				26,000			
P+L	Payroll expenses	31,150			150	31,000			
P+L	Purchases	188,000		900		188,900			
F	Payables ledger control account		29,900						29,900
P+L	Revenue		436,000				436,000		
F	Receivables ledger control account	36,000						36,000	
P+L	Selling expenses	67,000				67,000			
—	Suspense		250	1,150	900				
F	VAT		9,800						9,800
F	Vehicles at cost	62,000						62,000	
F	Vehicles accumulated depreciation		26,300		20,500				46,800
	Net profit					74,150			74,150
		508,080	508,080	63,150	63,150	476,600	476,600	165,880	165,880

402,450

63 GREENWOODS

You have the following extended trial balance. The adjustments have already been correctly entered. You now need to extend the figures into the statement of profit or loss and statement of financial position columns. Make the columns balance by entering figures and a label in the correct places.

Extended trial balance

Ledger account	Ledger balances		Adjustments		Statement of profit or loss		Statement of financial position	
	Dr £	Cr £	Dr £	Cr £	Dr £	Cr £	Dr £	Cr £
Accruals		2,300		425				*2,725*
Advertising	1,800				*1,800*			
Bank	7,912		1,175				*9,087*	
Capital		40,000						*40,000*
Closing inventory			6,590	6,590		*6,590*	*6,590*	
Depreciation charge			821		*821*			
Drawings	14,700						*14,700*	
Fixtures and fittings – accumulated depreciation		945		821				*1,766*
Fixtures and fittings – cost	6,099				*6,099*		*6,099*	
Interest	345				*345*			
Light and heat	1,587		706		*2,293*			
Loan		10,000						*10,000*
Opening inventory	5,215				*5,215*			
Prepayments	485		927	281			*1,131*	
Purchases	75,921				*75,921*			
PLCA		14,000						*14,000*
Rent and rates	38,000			927	*37,073*			
Revenue		145,825				*145,825*		
RLCA	9,500			1,175			*8,325*	
VAT control account		11,453						*11,453*
Wages	62,959				*62,959*			
					34,012	*34,012*		
	224,523	224,523	10,219	10,219	*186,427*	*186,427*	*79,944*	*79,944*

(Handwritten left-margin labels: F, PtL, F, F, Bxn, PtL, F, F, SFP PtL, PtL F, PtL, F, PtL, F, PtL, F, PtL, PtL, F, F, PtL)

64   WIDGETS

You work for Widgets, a business that makes and sells parts for kitchen appliances. You have been provided with an ETB that has been started by the current bookkeeper. However, the bookkeeper is now on holiday and the owner of Widgets has asked that you create the adjustments and enter them onto the ETB to save time.

Make the appropriate entries in the adjustments column of the extended trial balance to take account of the following. The year end date is 31 December 20X5.

(a)   The allowances for doubtful receivables figure is to be adjusted to 2% of receivables.

(b)   A credit note received from a supplier for goods returned was mislaid. It has since been found and has not yet been accounted for. It was for £2,000 net plus £400 VAT.

(c)   Rent is payable yearly in advance. For the 12 months to 31/10/X5 the rent is £12,000, the prepayment bought down has been included in the ledger balance. For the 12 months to 31/10/X6 the rent is £15,000.

(d)   Inventory is valued at cost at £14,890. However, there was a leak in the storage cupboard and £3,000 worth of items have been damaged and need to be written off.

(e)   The electricity bill of £450 for the 3 months ended 31 January 20X6 was received and paid in February 20X6.

Extended trial balance

Ledger account	Ledger balances		Adjustments	
	Dr £	Cr £	Dr £	Cr £
Accruals		1,330		
Advertising	1,800			
Bank	7,912			
Capital		50,000		
Closing inventory				
Depreciation charge				
Drawings	14,700			
Fixtures and fittings – accumulated depreciation		945		
Fixtures and fittings – cost	6,099			
Irrecoverable debts	345			
Allowance for doubtful receivables adjustment				
Electricity	1,587			
Loan	10,000			
Opening inventory	5,215			
Prepayment				
Allowance for doubtful receivables		485		
Purchases	78,921			
Purchase returns				2,000
PLCA		14,000		
Rent	25,000			
Revenue		145,825		
RLCA	9,500			
VAT control account		11,453		
Wages	62,959			
	224,038	224,038		

65 BINS 4 U

You work for Bins 4 U, a business that makes and sells glasses. You have been provided with an ETB that has been started by the current bookkeeper. However, the bookkeeper has left unexpectedly and the owner of Bins 4 U has asked that you create the adjustments and enter them onto the ETB.

Make the appropriate entries in the adjustments column of the extended trial balance to take account of the following. The year end date is 31 May 20X7.

(a) A credit note for a customer for goods returned was printed but never posted to the accounting system or to the customer. It was for £600 net plus £120 VAT.

(b) After considering part (a), the allowance for doubtful receivables is to be adjusted to 5% of the receivables balance.

(c) Rent is payable yearly in advance. For the 12 months to 31/3/X7 the rent is £6,000, the prepayment brought forward has been included in the ledger balances. For the 12 months to 31/3/X8 the rent is going to be £7,500.

(d) Inventory is valued at cost at £18,412. However, some items were sold after the year end for £2902 that originally cost £3,519.

(e) The water bill for the 3 months ended 31 July 20X7 was received and paid in August 20X7. The bill was for £180.

Extended trial balance

Ledger account	Ledger balances		Adjustments	
	Dr	Cr	Dr	Cr
	£	£	£	£
Accruals		2,900		
Administration expenses	900			
Allowance for doubtful receivables		1,040		
Bank overdraft		2,763		
Cash	246			
Capital		40,000		
Closing inventory				
Drawings	13,475			
Water	2,197			
Light and heat	2,018			
Loan		12,000		
Opening inventory	4,600			
Plant and machinery – accumulated depreciation		7,075		
Plant and machinery – cost	20,370			
Prepayments	1,200			
Purchases	100,159			
Rent	12,500			
Rates	8,500			
Salaries	46,376			
Revenue		151,606		
Sales returns				
RLCA	10,745			
Irrecoverable debts	850			
Allowance for doubtful receivables adjustments				
VAT control account		6,752		
	224,136	224,136		

66   TEAPOT

This task is about producing, adjusting, checking and extending the trial balance of a business, Teapot.

(a)   (i)   Identify whether the following balances are classified as debits or credits and appear within the statement of financial position or statement of profit or loss.

	Debit ✓	Credit ✓	Statement of financial position	Statement of profit or loss
Prepayments				
Discounts allowed				

(a)   (ii)   Complete the follow statements for each error identified below by selecting the appropriate word from the picklist available below.

Rental expenses incorrectly included within electricity expenses .... be identified by the initial trial balance.

The wrong economic lifetime used within the depreciation charges .... be identified by the initial trial balance.

A receipt from a credit customer which was correctly entered into the bank, but no other entries were made .... be identified by the initial trial balance.

Drawings during the year were debited to cash and to the drawings account .... be identified by the initial trial balance.

PICKLIST
will
will not

Alexa received her bank statement and has asked you to complete the bank reconciliation as at 31 March 20X8. The balance on the bank statement was £61.52 credit.

The cash book currently shows a debit balance of £191.52.

The following items are outstanding on either the bank statement or the cash book:

- Bank charges of £100 appear on the bank statement

- A wired bank transfer for £300 was received from Jacko Ltd. It appears on the bank statement but has not yet been entered into the cash book

- A cheque for £500 from JJ Nelli was received by Alexa and paid into the bank. The amount was included in the cash book but has not yet been recorded in the bank statement

- Alexa paid a cheque for £170 to Tony's Sweets Ltd just before the year end. This has not yet presented in the bank statement.

(b) **Produce the bank reconciliation statement. Show any overdrafts as negative figures. All other figures should be positive.**

Bank reconciliation as at 31 March 20X8	
	£
Balance as per the bank statement	
Add	
PICKLIST	
Less	
PICKLIST	
Balance as per the cash book	

PICKLIST
Bank charges
Jacko
JJ Nelli
Tony's Sweets

A trial balance has been produced for the year ended 31 March 20X8, which has total credits of £154,200 and total debits of £153,900.

(c) **Prepare the entries to correct the following errors using the blank journal below. Narratives are not required.**

- The closing balance of inventory has been omitted from the accounts. It is valued at £5,740.
- Alexa has decided to use some of her savings to expand the business. She paid a personal cheque into the business account for £5,000. This was posted to the correct accounts but the incorrect side of each account.
- A payment of £100 for electricity (no VAT) was correctly entered into the bank but omitted from the relevant expense account.
- The Total (gross) column of the Sales Returns Daybook was overcast by £200.

Account name	Debit £	Credit £
PICKLIST		
PICKLIST		
PICKLIST		
PICKLIST		
PICKLIST		
PICKLIST		
PICKLIST		
PICKLIST		

PICKLIST
Closing inventory: statement of financial position
Closing inventory: statement of profit or loss
Bank
Capital
Electricity
Suspense
Drawings
Payables ledger control account
Receivables ledger control account

(d)   Another client has asked you to help complete their business' extended trial balance. Fill in the missing information and ensure you calculate the profit or loss and specify in the appropriate space in the first column whether it is a profit or a loss.

Account name	Ledger balances		Adjustments		Statement of profit or loss		Statement of financial position	
	Dr	Cr	Dr	Cr	Dr	Cr	Dr	Cr
Payables ledger control		6,190						6,190
Receivables ledger control	525						525	
Value Added Tax		745						745
Bank	2,435						2,435	
Capital		15,000						15,000
Sales revenue		82,137				82,137		
Purchases	37,745			75	37,670			
Opening inventory	11,325							
Shop wages	21,212		210		21,422			
Accrued expenses				210				210
Heat and light	1,710				1,710			
Rent	6,340				6,340			
Prepayment of rent	375						375	
Closing inventory			12,710	12,710				
Shop fittings at cost	11,000		75				11,075	
Shop fittings: depreciation charges	2,625				2,625			
Shop fittings: accumulated depreciation		5,250						5,250
Loss on disposal of non-current asset	100							
Irrecoverable debts	60				60			
Drawings	13,870						13,870	
PICKLIST								
Total	109,322	109,322	12,995	12,995				

PICKLIST
Profit for the year
Loss for the year

67   RZ TRAINING

This task is about producing, adjusting, checking and extending the trial balance of a business, Coffeepot.

(a)   (i)   Identify whether the following statements about extended trial balances are true or false.

Statement	True ✓	False ✓
Opening inventory will be included in both the statement of profit or loss and statement of financial position columns.		
Drawings will be in the credit column of the statement of financial position.		
Losses for the year will be shown in the credit column within the statement of profit or loss.		
The total of debits and credits in the adjustment columns will be equal.		

Jakki runs RZ Training which is not VAT registered.

(ii)   State the overall effect on the elements on the accounting equation for each of these transactions.

Statement	Assets	Liabilities	Capital
RZ Training buys computer equipment for cash	PICKLIST	PICKLIST	PICKLIST
Jakki withdrew cash from RZ Training to buy her daughter a new puppy	PICKLIST	PICKLIST	PICKLIST

PICKLIST
Increase
Decrease
No effect

You are reconciling the balance on the payables' ledger control account to the sum of the balances on the individual accounts within the payables ledger.

The payables' ledger control account balance	£82,338
The sum of the balances on the individual payable accounts	£81,642

Following an investigation, a number of errors have been discovered.

(b) **Identify the entries which need to be made in the relevant accounts to correct any errors that may have caused the difference between the two balances.**

Each error should have at least one entry next to it. If there is no overall effect, place a tick in the 'No effect' column.

Errors	Payables Ledger control account		Individual payables accounts		No effect
	Debit £	Credit £	Debit £	Credit £	
A credit note from Jasmine Gubta for £422.10 (including VAT) has been posted to Josh Grealish's account in the payables ledger.					
A credit note for discount received of £36 (including VAT) has been entered into Declan Curry's individual account but has been omitted from the payables' ledger control account completely.					
In the payables' ledger, a purchase invoice for £180 including VAT was posted to the wrong side of G Southfence's account.					
The total column in the purchases daybook has been overcast by £300.					

The ledger columns of the extended trial balance for M Wie has been produced for the year ended 31 March 20X8.

The debit column totalled £5,347,730 and the credit column totalled £5,348,730, so a suspense account was set up.

(c) **Correct the following errors by entering the adjustments required into the extended trial balance.**

- The accounting entries for a bank payment for rent of £9,600 was recorded in the correct accounts, but the accounting entries had been reversed (no VAT is applicable).
- The total column in the sales daybook was overcast by £2,000.

- M Wie paid £3,000 to P Mickelson, a supplier, to settle the amount owed. This was recorded in the cash book only.
- No entry has been made for closing inventory of £16,856.

Trial Balance for M Wie as at 31 March 20X8				
	Ledger balances		Adjustments	
	Dr	Cr	Dr	Cr
	£	£	£	£
Accumulated depreciation		447,938		
Administration expenses	739,800			
Cash at bank	33,946			
Capital		1,494,522		
Depreciation charge	54,900			
Wages	821,074			
Drawings	77,818			
Irrecoverable debts	2,738			
Non-current assets at cost	2,178,348			
Opening inventory	17,338			
Other expenses	708,958			
Purchases	420,886			
Rent	170,894			
Sales revenue		3,251,284		
VAT		60,512		
Trade payables		94,474		
Trade receivables	121,030			
Closing inventory SFP				
Closing inventory SPL				
Suspense	1,000			
	5,348,730	5,348,730		

You have now been asked to complete the trial balance of a business as at 31 March 20X9, an extract of which is shown below.

You are given the following information:

- Deferred income for the year has been estimated at £500. The allowance for doubtful receivables figure has increased by £50 and is now £900.

- Due to the sale of a non-current asset last month, there is a VAT liability of £270.

- During the year a non-current asset was sold, which resulted in a loss of £125.

- The business received prompt payment discounts from its suppliers of £910 during the year.

(d)   Complete the trial balance extract.

Extract of the trial balance as at 31 March 20X9		
	Dr £	Cr £
Deferred income		
Allowance for doubtful receivables		
VAT		
Discount received		
Loss on disposal of NCA		
Increase in allowance for doubtful receivables		

68   CAFETIERE

This task is about producing, adjusting, checking and extending the trial balance of a business, Cafetiere.

(a)   (i)   Identify whether the following balances are classified as debits or credits and whether they are included within the statement of financial position or statement of profit or loss.

	Debit ✓	Credit ✓	Statement of financial position ✓	Statement of profit or loss ✓
Bank overdraft				
Capital introduced				

(ii)   Identify whether each of the following statements are true or false.

Statement	True ✓	False ✓
In the statement of profit or loss columns in the extended trial balance, If the debits column is larger than the credits column, the business has made a profit for the year.		
In a bank reconciliation, outstanding lodgements will cause the bank statement to be higher than the cash book balance.		
VAT on purchase returns will be credited to the VAT control account.		
In a partnership, the appropriation of profit will be credited to the partners' capital accounts.		

You are reconciling the balance on the receivables' ledger control account to the sum of the balances on the individual accounts within the receivables' ledger.

The receivables' ledger control account balance   £163,632

The sum of the balance on the individual receivable accounts   £163,284

Following an investigation, a number of errors have been discovered which are noted below.

(b) **Identify the entries which need to be made in the relevant accounts to correct any errors that may have caused the difference between the two balances.**

Each error should have at least one entry next to it. If there is no overall effect, place a tick in the 'No effect' column.

Errors	Receivables ledger control account		Individual receivables accounts		No effect ✓
	Debit £	Credit £	Debit £	Credit £	
An invoice of £72 has been entered twice in D Asher-Smith's individual account.					
In the receivables ledger, an invoice for £360 was posted to the wrong side of S Cram's account.					
A credit note to M. Farah for £130 has been posted to J Ennis' account in the receivables ledger.					
The total column in the sales daybook has been undercast by £300.					

The trial balance for a business has been produced for the year ended 31 March 20X8. It had total debits of £308,400, and total credits of £309,100.

(c)   Prepare the entries to correct the following errors using the blank journal below. Narratives are not required.

- The closing balance of inventory has been omitted from the accounts. It is valued at £11,480

- Cash was received from a credit customer of £10,000. This has been posted to the correct accounts but to the incorrect side of each account.

- An accrual of £500 for broadband has been correctly entered in the statement of financial position as an accrual but omitted from the relevant expense account.

- The Total (gross) column of the Purchases Daybook has been overcast by £200.

Account name	Debit £	Credit £
PICKLIST		
PICKLIST		
PICKLIST		
PICKLIST		
PICKLIST		
PICKLIST		
PICKLIST		
PICKLIST		

PICKLIST
Closing inventory: statement of financial position
Closing inventory: statement of profit or loss
Bank
Capital
Broadband expense
Suspense
Drawings
Payables ledger control account
Receivables ledger control account

You have now been asked to complete the trial balance as at 31 March 20X9, an extract of which is shown below.

You are given the following information:

- Prepayments at the year-end have been calculated as £250. The allowance for doubtful receivables balance is £1,000. Last year, the allowance for doubtful receivables was £1,500.

- Due to a large purchase of a non-current asset last month, the business is now owed £600 in respect of VAT.

- During the year there was a disposal of a non-current asset, which resulted in a gain of £160. The entity was also given prompt payment discounts by its suppliers of £200 during the year.

(d) **Complete the trial balance extract.**

Trial balance extract as at 31 March 20X9		
	Dr £	Cr £
Prepayments		
Allowance for doubtful receivables		
VAT		
Discount received		
Gain on disposal of NCA		
Movement in allowance for doubtful receivables		

PRODUCE FINANCIAL STATEMENTS FOR SOLE TRADERS AND PARTNERSHIPS

69 PG TRADING

You have the following trial balance for a sole trader known as PG Trading. All the necessary year-end adjustments have been made.

PG Trading has a policy of showing trade receivables net of any allowance for doubtful receivables.

The statement of profit or loss for PG Trading shows a profit of £7,900 for the period.

(a) **Prepare a statement of financial position for the business for the year ended 30 September 20X7.**

PG Trading		
Trial balance as at 30 September 20X7		
	Dr £	**Cr** £
Accruals		6,000
Bank	5,000	
Capital		20,000
Drawings	3,000	
Closing inventory	11,000	11,000
Depreciation charge	1,800	
Allowance for doubtful receivables adjustment	800	
General expenses	6,400	
Machinery at cost	15,900	
Machinery accumulated depreciation		5,800
Opening inventory	9,800	
Prepayments	5,100	
Allowance for doubtful receivables		800
Purchases	46,000	
Payables ledger control account		15,900
Rent	12,000	
Sales		78,700
Receivables ledger control account	17,900	
VAT		1,500
Wages	5,000	
	139,700	139,700

PG Trading			
Statement of financial position as at 30 September 20X7			
	£	£	£
Non-current assets	**Cost**	**Depreciation**	**Carrying amount**
Current assets			
Current liabilities			
Net current assets			
Net assets			
Financed by:			
Opening capital			
Add:			
Less:			
Closing capital			

(b)   Using your answer to part (a), what will be the opening capital balance on 1 October 20X7?

£_____

70   INVENTORY TRADING

You have the following trial balance for a sole trader known as Inventory Trading. All the necessary year-end adjustments have been made.

Inventory Trading has a policy of showing trade receivables net of any allowance for doubtful receivables.

The statement of profit or loss for Inventory Trading shows a profit of £15,000 for the period.

(a)   **Prepare a statement of financial position for the business for the year ended 31 March 20X1.**

Inventory Trading		
Trial balance as at 31 March 20X1		
	Dr **£**	**Cr** **£**
Accruals		2,500
Administration expenses	40,000	
Bank	4,100	
Capital		74,390
Cash	670	
Closing inventory	20,000	20,000
Drawings	1,400	
Depreciation charge	3,600	
Disposal of non-current asset	3,500	
Motor vehicles at cost	39,000	
Motor vehicles accumulated depreciation		18,500
Opening inventory	25,400	
Allowance for doubtful receivables		1,200
Allowance for doubtful receivables adjustment	110	
Purchases	83,300	
Payables ledger control account		28,500
Revenue		156,800
Receivables ledger control account	78,920	
Selling expenses	5,890	
VAT		4,000
Total	305,890	305,890

Inventory Trading			
Statement of financial position as at 31 March 20X1			
	£	£	£
Non-current assets	**Cost**	**Depreciation**	**Carrying amount**
Current assets			
Current liabilities			
Net current assets			
Net assets			
Financed by:			
Opening capital			
Add:			
Less:			
Closing capital			

(b) If there had been a prepayment balance in the trial balance, where would this be shown in the statement of financial position? Choose one option.

- As a non-current asset.
- As a current liability.
- In the 'financed by' section.
- As a current asset.

71 WINSTON TRADING

You have the following trial balance for a sole trader known as Winston Trading. All the necessary year-end adjustments have been made.

Winston Trading has a policy of showing trade receivables net of any allowance for doubtful receivables and showing trade payables and sundry payables as one total figure.

The statement of profit or loss for Winston Trading shows a profit of £8,810 for the period.

Prepare a statement of financial position for the business for the year ended 30 June 20X8.

Winston Trading		
Trial balance as at 30 June 20X8		
	Dr **£**	**Cr** **£**
Accruals		750
Bank		1,250
Capital		17,000
Closing inventory	7,850	7,850
Discounts received		900
Sundry payables		1,450
Payables ledger control account		6,800
Depreciation charge	1,600	
Discounts allowed	345	
Allowance for doubtful receivables adjustment	295	
Equipment accumulated depreciation		4,500
Wages	24,000	
Receivables ledger control account	7,800	
Rent	5,250	
Revenue		164,000
Disposal		450
Prepayments	3,200	
Purchases	125,000	
Sales returns	1,500	
Opening inventory	3,450	
Equipment at cost	17,500	
Drawings	8,000	
General expenses	2,950	
Allowance for doubtful receivables		840
VAT		2,950
	208,740	208,740

Winston Trading			
Statement of financial position as at 30 June 20X8			
	£	£	£
Non-current assets	**Cost**	**Depreciation**	**Carrying amount**
Current assets			
Current liabilities			
Net current assets			
Net assets			
Financed by:			
Opening capital			
Add:			
Less:			
Closing capital			

72 BALFOUR

You are preparing the statement of financial position for Balfour, a sole trader. All the necessary year-end adjustments have been made.

Balfour has a policy of showing trade receivables net of any allowance for doubtful receivables. The statement of profit or loss for Balfour shows a loss of £4,350 for the period.

Prepare a statement of financial position for the business for the year ended 30 June 20X6.

| **Balfour** | | |
| **Trial balance as at 30 June 20X6** | | |
	Dr **£**	**Cr** **£**
Accruals		3,150
Administration expenses	45,000	
Bank		2,250
Capital		85,000
Cash	500	
Closing inventory	17,500	17,500
Depreciation charge	9,000	
Disposal of non-current asset		1,500
Motor vehicles at cost	45,000	
Motor vehicles accumulated depreciation		20,000
Opening inventory	15,000	
Allowance for doubtful receivables		1,450
Allowance for doubtful receivables adjustment	200	
Purchases	75,000	
Payables ledger control account		23,750
Revenue		130,000
Receivables ledger control account	68,550	
Selling expenses	9,150	
Drawings	3,200	
VAT		3,500
Total	288,100	288,100

Balfour			
Statement of financial position as at 30 June 20X6			
	£	£	£
Non-current assets	**Cost**	**Depreciation**	**Carrying amount**
Current assets			
Current liabilities			
Net current assets			
Net assets			
Financed by:			
Opening capital			
Less:			
Less:			
Closing capital			

73   ROG

This task is about final accounts for sole traders.

The following are accounting policies used by ROG:

- Sales revenue should include sales returns, if any.

- Purchases should include purchases returns and carriage inwards, if any.

You have the following trial balance for a sole trader known as ROG. All the necessary year-end adjustments have been made.

(a)   (i)   Calculate the sales figure to be included in the statement of profit or loss for ROG.

£_____

(ii)   Calculate the purchases figure to be included in the statement of profit or loss for ROG.

£_____

Trial balance of ROG for the year ended 31 March 20X7.	Dr £	Cr £
Capital		55,000
Drawings	22,000	
Plant and machinery – Cost	50,000	
Plant and machinery – Accumulated depreciation		27,600
Motor vehicle – Cost	15,000	
Motor vehicle – Accumulated depreciation		3,000
Closing inventory – Statement of financial position	3,480	
Closing inventory – Statement of profit or loss		3,480
Prepaid expenses	890	
Accrued expenses		1,000
Payables ledger control account		6,000
Revenue		160,150
Bank	20,000	
Cash in hand	5,000	
Rent	7,200	
Payroll expenses	14,000	
Sales returns	5,150	
Receivables ledger control account	29,380	
Purchases	71,170	
Allowance for doubtful receivables adjustment	220	
Allowance for doubtful receivables		1,600
Advertising	2,000	
Miscellaneous expenses	1,500	
Disposal		320
Depreciation charges	6,600	
Opening inventory	2,980	
Carriage inwards	1,580	
Total	**258,150**	**258,150**

(b) **Prepare a statement of profit or loss for ROG for the year ended 31 March 20X7.**

If necessary, ONLY use a minus sign to indicate the following:

- the deduction of an account balance from cost of sales

- a loss for the year.

Statement of profit or loss for ROG for the year ended 31 March 20X7.

	£	£
Revenue		
Cost of sales		
Gross profit		
Sundry income		
Expenses		
Total expenses		
Profit/(loss) for the year		

You have the following information about a different sole trader for the year ended 31 March 20X8:

- A loss of £15,500 was recorded.

- The proprietor of the business took £2,800 out of the business to pay personal expenses.

- The proprietor did not invest any further capital.

(c)   Complete the capital account below for the year ended 31 March 20X8, clearly showing the balance carried down.

Capital

	£		£
		Balance b/d	42,000
Total		Total	

74   OLIVIA

This task is about final accounts for sole traders.

The following are accounting policies used by Olivia:

- Sales revenue should include sales returns, if any.

- Purchases should include purchases returns and carriage inwards, if any.

You have the following trial balance for a sole trader, Olivia. All the necessary year-end adjustments have been made.

(a)   (i)   Calculate the sales figure to be included in the statement of profit or loss for Olivia.

£_____

(ii)   Calculate the purchases figure to be included in the statement of profit or loss for Olivia.

£_____

Trial balance of Olivia for the year ended 31 March 20X7.

	Dr £	Cr £
Sales		704,440
Purchases	400,746	
Opening inventory	41,211	
Payroll expenses	113,326	
General expenses	72,900	
Motor expenses	14,633	
Allowance for doubtful receivables adjustment		750
Sales returns	15,220	
Allowance for doubtful receivables		2,675
Purchases returns		12,885
Motor vehicles – Cost	37,400	
Motor vehicles – Accumulated depreciation		19,160
Fixtures and fittings – Cost	46,100	
Fixtures and fittings – Accumulated depreciation		20,855
Capital		64,000
Drawings	40,000	
Receivables ledger control account	60,367	
Payables ledger control account		55,812
Bank	26,338	
VAT		4,529
Closing inventory	64,500	64,500
Disposal	3,870	
Depreciation charges	12,995	
	949,606	**949,606**

(b) **Prepare a statement of profit or loss for Olivia for the year ended 31 March 20X7.**

If necessary, ONLY use a minus sign to indicate the following:

- the deduction of an account balance from cost of sales

- a loss for the year.

Statement of profit or loss for Olivia for the year ended 31 March 20X7.

	£	£
Revenue		
Cost of sales		
Gross profit		
Sundry income		
Expenses		
Total expenses		
Profit/(loss) for the year		

(c)   You have the following information about another sole trader, JOR, for the year ended 31 December 20X7.

The proprietor of JOR removed goods from the business during the year, they were valued at £680.

What affect would this have on each of the following?

	Increase ✓	Decrease ✓	No change ✓
Assets			
Liabilities			
Capital			

75 RACHAEL, ED AND MATTY

You have the following information about a partnership business:

The financial year ends on 30 June.

- The partners are Rachael, Ed and Matty.

- Partners' annual salaries

  Rachael £18,000, – Ed nil, – Matty   £36,000

- Partners' interest on capital (per annum)

  Rachael £2,000, Ed £2,000, Matty £2,000

- Partners' sales commission earned during the year

  Rachael £8,250, Ed £6,800, Matty £4,715

- Profit share

  Rachael 40%, Ed 40%, Matty 20%

The statement of profit or loss for the partnership shows a profit for the year ended 30 June 20X9 of £220,000 before appropriations.

Prepare the appropriation account for the partnership for the year ended 30 June 20X9. Any profit figures should be shown as positive and any losses should be shown using a minus sign as negative. All other figures should be shown as positive. If any figure is zero enter 0.

Partnership Appropriation account for the year ended 30 June 20X9

	£
Profit for the year	
Salaries:	
Rachael	
Ed	
Matty	
Interest on capital:	
Rachael	
Ed	
Matty	
Sales commission:	
Rachael	
Ed	
Matty	
Profit available for distribution	

Profit share:	
Rachael	
Ed	
Matty	
Total residual profit distributed	

76 NYAH, SHAUNA AND MOLLIE

You have the following information about a partnership business:

- The financial year ends on 31 March.

- The partners are Nyah, Shauna and Mollie.

- Partners' annual salaries

    - Nyah   £25,000

    - Shauna   £19,000

    - Mollie   nil

- Partners' sales commission earned during the year

    - Nyah   £1,100 per annum

    - Shauna   £1,100 per annum

    - Mollie   £1,100 per annum

- Profit share

    - Nyah   35%

    - Shauna   20%

    - Mollie   45%

The statement of profit or loss for the partnership shows a profit for the year ended 31 March 20Y0 of £70,000 before appropriations.

Prepare the appropriation account for the partnership for the year ended 31 March 20Y0. Any profit figures should be shown as positive and any losses should be shown using a minus sign as negative. All other figures should be shown as positive. If any figure is zero enter 0.

Partnership Appropriation account for the year ended 31 March 20Y0

	£
Profit for the year	
Salaries:	
Nyah	
Shauna	
Mollie	
Sales commission	
Nyah	
Shauna	
Mollie	
Profit available for distribution	

Profit share:	
Nyah	
Shauna	
Mollie	
Total residual profit distributed	

77 EDWARD, JAKE AND BELLA

This task is about partnership accounts. You have the following information about a partnership business:

- The financial year ends on 31 December.
- The partners are Edward, Jake and Bella.
- Partners' annual salaries

  Edward £30,000, Jake nil, Bella £21,000
- Partners' sales commission earned during the year

  Edward £3,000 per annum, Jake £3,000 per annum, Bella £3,200 per annum
- Partners' interest on drawings

  Edward £1,880 per annum, Jake £2,870 per annum, Bella nil
- Profit share

  Edward 50%. Jake 20%, Bella 30%

Profit for the year for the year ended 31 December 20X0 was £52,000 before appropriations.

Prepare the appropriation account for the partnership for the year ended 31 December 20X0. Any profit figures should be shown as positive and any losses should be shown using a minus sign as negative. All other figures should be shown as positive. If any figure is zero enter 0.

Partnership Appropriation account for the year ended 31 December 20X0

	£
Profit for the year	
Salaries:	
Edward	
Jake	
Bella	
Sales commission:	
Edward	
Jake	
Bella	
Interest on drawings:	
Edward	
Jake	
Bella	
Residual profit / loss	

Profit / loss share:	
Edward	
Jake	
Bella	
Total residual profit / loss distributed	

78 GARY, MARK AND ROBBIE

Gary, Mark and Robbie are in partnership, preparing accounts to the year ended 30 June. You are given the following information:

- The financial year ends on 30 June.

- Partners' annual salaries

  Gary £18,000, Mark nil, Robbie £36,000

- Partners' capital account balances as at 30 June 20X9

  Gary £100,000, Mark £60,000, Robbie £75,000

- Partners' interest on capital for the year

  Gary £5,000, Mark £3,000, Robbie £3,750

- The partners share the remaining profit of £80,000 as follows:

  Gary 40%, Mark 40%, Robbie 20%

- Partners' drawings for the year

  Gary £34,000, Mark £30,000, Robbie £58,000

Prepare the current accounts for the partners for the year ended 30 June 20X9, showing clearly the balances carried down.

Current accounts

	Gary £	Mark £	Robbie £		Gary £	Mark £	Robbie £
				Balance b/d	2,000	1,500	250

79 JOHN, JACKIE AND TEGAN

John, Jackie and Tegan are in partnership, producing accounts to the year ended 30 June. You are given the following information:

- Partners' annual salaries
    - John   £11,000
    - Jackie   £16,500
    - Tegan   nil

- Partners' capital account balances as at 30 June 20X8
    - John   £47,500
    - Jackie   £56,000
    - Tegan   £56,000

- Partners' interest on capital for the year
    - John   £1,900
    - Jackie   £2,240
    - Tegan   £2,240

- The partners share the **remaining** profit of £75,000 as follows:
    - John   35%
    - Jackie   45%
    - Tegan   20%

- Partners' drawings for the year
    - John   £18,000
    - Jackie   £35,000
    - Tegan   £12,750

Prepare the current accounts for the partners for the year ended 30 June 20X8. Show clearly the balances carried down.

Current accounts

	John £	Jackie £	Tegan £		John £	Jackie £	Tegan £
Balance b/d	750			Balance b/d		1,900	600

80 LOUIS, CHERYL AND SIMON

Louis, Cheryl and Simon are in partnership producing accounts to the year ended 31 December. You are given the following information:

- Partners' annual salaries

    - Louis   £30,000

    - Cheryl   nil

    - Simon   £21,000

- Partners' capital account balances as at 31 December 20X9

    - Louis   £50,000

    - Cheryl   £50,000

    - Simon   £20,000

- Partners' interest on capital for the year

    - Louis   £1,000

    - Cheryl   £1,000

    - Simon   £400

- The partners share the remaining profit of £60,000 as follows:

    - Louis   50%

    - Cheryl   20%

    - Simon   30%

- Partners' drawings for the year

    - Louis   £25,000

    - Cheryl   £10,200

    - Simon   £31,000

Prepare the current accounts for the partners for the year ended 31 December 20X9. Show clearly the balances carried down.

Current accounts

	Louis £	Cheryl £	Simon £		Louis £	Cheryl £	Simon £
				Balance b/d	3,500	1,800	1,000

81   DEREK, JIN AND AHMED

Derek, Jin and Ahmed are in business together sharing profits in the ratio 3:3:4 after providing for salaries for Derek and Jin of £20,000 and £24,000 respectively. The partners each receive interest on their capital balances and pay interest of on their drawings as outlined below. The profit for the year to 31 March 20X8 is £254,000 before providing for salaries or interest.

	Interest on capital	Interest on drawings
	£	£
Derek	8,000	4,600
Jin	7,200	3,800
Ahmed	10,560	4,800

Prepare the appropriation account for the partnership for the year ended 31 March 20X8. Any profit figures should be shown as positive and any losses should be shown using a minus sign as negative. All other figures should be shown as positive. If any figure is zero enter 0.

Partnership Appropriation account for the year ended 31 March 20X8

	£
Profit for the year	
Salaries:	
Derek	
Jin	
Ahmed	
Interest on capital:	
Derek	
Jin	
Ahmed	
Interest on drawings:	
Derek	
Jin	
Ahmed	
Profit available for distribution	

	£
Profit share:	
Derek	
Jin	
Ahmed	
Total residual profit distributed	

82   JACOB AND OLIVER

Jacob and Oliver are in partnership sharing profits equally and compiling financial statements to 31 December each year. They are both paid a salary of £20,000 each year. They receive both interest on their capital balances, sales commission on their sales made during the year and pay interest on their drawings which are all outlined below:

	Interest on capital	Interest on drawings	Sales commission earned
	£	£	£
Jacob	2,800	2,275	1,560
Oliver	6,250	0	2,690

The profit for the year ended 31 December 20X8 is £182,225 before appropriations.

Prepare the appropriation account for the partnership for the year ended 31 December 20X8. Any profit figures should be shown as positive and any losses should be shown using a minus sign as negative. All other figures should be shown as positive. If any figure is zero enter 0.

Partnership Appropriation account for the year ended 31 December 20X8:

	£
Profit for the year	
Salaries:	
Jacob	
Oliver	
Interest on capital:	
Jacob	
Oliver	
Sales commission:	
Jacob	
Oliver	
Interest on drawings:	
Jacob	
Oliver	
Profit available for distribution	

	£
Profit share:	
Jacob	
Oliver	
Total residual profit distributed	

83 R & R TRADING

You have the following trial balance for a partnership known as R & R Trading. All the necessary year-end adjustments have been made.

The partners are Rita and Richard; they share profits 55:45 with Rita taking the larger share.

R & R Trading have a policy of including sales returns in the sales figure and purchases returns in the purchases figure.

Use a minus sign to indicate the following ONLY:

- a net loss for the year
- the closing inventory figure.

(a) **Prepare a statement of profit or loss for the business for the year ended 30 September 20X7.**

R & R Trading Trial balance as at 30 September 20X7		
	Dr **£**	**Cr** **£**
Accruals		4,100
Bank	3,500	
Closing inventory	19,500	19,500
Capital – Rita		5,050
Capital – Richard		5,050
Current– Rita		920
Current – Richard	745	
Depreciation charge	7,100	
Discounts allowed	1,350	
Drawings – Rita	6,000	
Drawings – Richard	5,000	
General expenses	26,100	
Machinery at cost	26,175	
Machinery accumulated depreciation		15,000
Opening inventory	17,700	
Sales returns	2,200	
Prepayments	4,600	
Purchases	98,000	
Payables ledger control account		32,000
Rent	7,300	
Revenue		173,050
Receivables ledger control account	26,400	
VAT		5,500
Wages	8,500	
	260,170	260,170

R & R Trading		
Statement of profit or loss for the year ended 30 September 20X7		
	£	£
Revenue		
Cost of goods sold		
Gross profit		
Less:		
Total expenses		
Profit for the year		

(b) **Calculate Rita's share of the profit or loss and her final current account balance.**

	£
Rita's share of the profit or loss	
Rita's final current account balance	

84 OSMOND PARTNERSHIP

You have the following trial balance for a partnership known as Osmond Partnership. All the necessary year-end adjustments have been made.

The partners are Aimee and Heather who share profits and losses equally.

Osmond Partnership have a policy of including sales returns in the sales figure and purchases returns in the purchases figure.

Use a minus sign to indicate the following ONLY:

- a net loss for the year

- the closing inventory figure.

(a) Prepare a statement of profit or loss for the partnership for the year ended 31 March 20X1.

Osmond Partnership Trial balance as at 31 March 20X1		
	Dr £	Cr £
Accruals		750
Bank		1,250
Capital – Aimee		8,000
Capital – Heather		7,500
Closing inventory	7,850	7,850
Discounts received		900
Current – Aimee		1,000
Current – Heather	400	
Sundry payables		1,450
Payables ledger control account		6,800
Depreciation charge	1,600	
Discounts allowed	345	
Irrecoverable debt expense	295	
Drawings – Aimee	3,250	
Drawings – Heather	3,250	
Allowance for doubtful receivables		840
Equipment at cost	18,100	
Equipment accumulated depreciation		4,500
Prepayments	3,200	
Receivables ledger control account	7,800	
Wages	24,000	
Rent	5,250	
Disposal		450
Sales returns	1,500	
Opening inventory	3,450	
Purchases	125,000	
General expenses	2,950	
Revenue		164,000
VAT		2,950
	208,240	208,240

Osmond Partnership		
Statement of profit or loss for the year ended 31 March 20X1		
	£	£
Revenue		
Cost of goods sold		
Gross profit		
Add:		
Total sundry income		
Less:		
Total expenses		
Profit for the year		

(b)   **Using your answer to part (a), calculate Heather's share of the profit or loss and her final current account balance.**

	£
Heather's share of the profit or loss	
Heather's final current account balance	

85   PERSEPHONE'S

You are preparing the statement of profit or loss for Persephone's for the year ended 30 June 20X8.

The partners are Tina and Cher. They share profits and losses 60:40, with Tina taking the larger share.

All the necessary year-end adjustments have been made.

Use a minus sign to indicate the following ONLY:

*   a net loss for the year

*   the closing inventory figure.

(a) Using the trial balance provided, prepare a statement of profit or loss for the partnership for the year ended 30 June 20X8.

Persephone's

Trial balance as at 30 June 20X8

	Dr £	Cr £
Accruals		2,500
Bank	3,500	
Capital – Tina		2,050
Capital – Cher		2,050
Closing inventory	9,800	9,800
Depreciation charge	800	
Allowance for doubtful receivables adjustment		1,000
Current – Tina		2,257
Current – Cher		3,750
Drawings – Tina	2,054	
Drawings – Cher	2,553	
General expenses	8,200	
Machinery at cost	10,500	
Machinery accumulated depreciation		4,300
Opening inventory	9,100	
Prepayments	6,100	
Purchases	38,700	
Payables ledger control account		12,500
Rent	5,900	
Revenue		85,000
Allowance for doubtful receivables		1,850
Receivables ledger control account	23,350	
VAT		2,000
Wages	8,500	
	129,057	129,057

Persephone's		
Statement of profit or loss for the year ended 30 June 20X8		
	£	£
Revenue		
Cost of goods sold		
Gross profit		
Plus:		
Less:		
Total expenses		
Profit for the year		

(b) Calculate Tina's and Cher's closing current account balances in the table below as well as showing their capital balances.

	Tina (£)	Cher (£)	Total (£)
Current account			
Capital account			

86 SUAREZ PARTNERSHIP

You are preparing the statement of profit or loss for the Suarez Partnership for the year ended 30 June 20X6. The partners are Louis and Emilio. They share profits equally.

All the necessary year-end adjustments have been made. Suarez Partnership have a policy of including sales returns in the sales figure and purchases returns in the purchases figure.

Use a minus sign to indicate the following ONLY:

- a net loss for the year
- the closing inventory figure.

(a) **Prepare a statement of profit or loss for the partnership for the year ended 30 June 20X6.**

Suarez Partnership

Trial balance as at 30 June 20X6

	Dr £	Cr £
Accruals		1,375
Bank		900
Capital – Louis		4,160
Capital – Emilio		3,000
Closing inventory	12,500	12,500
Depreciation charge	925	
Disposal of non-current asset		225
Drawings – Louis	2,500	
Drawings – Emilio	2,500	
Current – Louis		1,500
Current – Emilio	200	
General expenses	9,300	
Machinery at cost	8,000	
Machinery accumulated depreciation		5,200
Opening inventory	13,100	
Prepayments	1,250	
Purchases	70,600	
Purchases returns		2,350
Payables ledger control account		11,375
Rent	6,000	
Revenue		108,000
Receivables ledger control account	17,800	
VAT		6,090
Wages	12,000	
	156,675	156,675

Suarez Partnership		
Statement of profit or loss for the year ended 30 June 20X6		
	£	£
Revenue		
Cost of goods sold		
Gross profit		
Plus:		
Less:		
Total expenses		
Profit for the year		

(b) Calculate Louis' and Emilio's closing current account balances in the table below as well as showing their capital balances.

	Louis (£)	Emilio (£)	Total (£)
Current account			
Capital account			

87 JCR PARTNERSHIP

This task is about preparing final accounts for a partnership.

You are preparing the statement of financial position for the JCR partnership as at 31 March 20X7.

The partners are June and Charlie.

You have the trial balance below. All the necessary year-end adjustments have been made, except for the transfer of £31,970 profit to the partners' current accounts. Partners share profits and losses 3:2 with June taking the larger share.

Using the information, complete the following tasks:

(i) **Calculate the partners' current account balances after sharing profits. You should show whether the balance is a credit or debit balance.**

	Balance	Debit	Credit
June	£		
Charlie	£		

JCR partnership has a policy of netting receivables and allowance for doubtful receivables against each other.

(ii) **Calculate the receivables figure to appear in the statement of financial position for JCR partnership.**

£_____

JCR partnership		
Trial balance as at 31 March 20X7		
	Dr **£**	**Cr** **£**
Accrued expenses		4,080
Bank	4,000	
Closing inventory	22,000	22,000
Capital – June		7,000
Capital – Charlie		5,000
Current– June		900
Current – Charlie	680	
Depreciation charges	8,000	
Discounts allowed	1,350	
Drawings – June	6,000	
Drawings – Charlie	5,000	
General expenses	24,820	
Machinery at cost	35,176	
Machinery accumulated depreciation		15,220
Opening inventory	17,700	
Sales returns	2,200	
Prepaid expenses	5,414	
Purchases	98,000	
Payables ledger control account		32,000
Rent	7,300	
Revenue		178,400
Receivables ledger control account	26,400	
VAT		5,500
Allowance for doubtful receivables		3,000
Allowance for doubtful receivables adjustment	560	
Wages	8,500	
	273,100	**273,100**

(iii) Prepare the statement of financial position for the partnership as at 31 March 20X7. Use the figures from the trial balance and the figures calculated above. DO NOT use brackets or minus signs.

JCR

Statement of financial position as at 31 March 20X7.

	£	£	£
Non-current assets	Cost	Accumulated depreciation	Carrying amount
Current assets			
Current liabilities			
Net current assets			
Net assets			
Financed by:			
	June	Charlie	Total

88   FORCE PARTNERSHIP

This task is about preparing final accounts for a partnership.

You are preparing the statement of financial position for the FORCE partnership as at 31 March 20X7. The partners are Tracey and Matilda.

You have the trial balance below. All the necessary year-end adjustments have been made, except for the transfer of £5,695 loss to the partners' current accounts. Partners share profits and losses 2:1 with Tracey taking the larger share.

Using the information, complete the following tasks:

(i)   **Calculate the partners' current account balances after sharing profits. You should show whether the balance is a credit or debit balance.**

	Balance	Debit	Credit
Tracey	£		
Matilda	£		

FORCE partnership has a policy of netting receivables and allowance for doubtful receivables against each other.

(ii)   **Calculate the receivables figure to appear in the statement of financial position for FORCE partnership.**

£_____

FORCE Partnership Trial balance as at 31 March 20X7	Dr £	Cr £
Accrued expenses		750
Bank		1,250
Capital – Tracey		18,000
Capital – Matilda		17,500
Closing inventory	6,500	6,500
Discounts received		900
Current – Tracey		1,000
Current – Matilda	400	
Payables ledger control account		6,800
Depreciation charges	1,600	
Discounts allowed	345	
Allowance for doubtful receivables adjustment	400	
Drawings – Tracey	3,250	
Drawings – Matilda	3,250	
Allowance for doubtful receivables		840
Equipment at cost	18,100	
Equipment accumulated depreciation		4,500
Prepaid expenses	3,200	
Receivables ledger control account	27,800	
Wages	26,000	
Rent	5,250	
Disposal	450	
Sales returns	1,500	
Opening inventory	4,600	
Purchases	134,000	
General expenses	2,950	
Revenue		164,000
VAT		17,555
	239,595	239,595

(iii) **Prepare the statement of financial position for the partnership as at 31 March 20X7. Use the figures from the trial balance and the figures calculated above. DO NOT use brackets or minus signs.**

FORCE

Statement of financial position as at 31 March 20X7.

	£	£	£
Non-current assets	Cost	Accumulated depreciation	Carrying amount
Current assets			
Current liabilities			
Net current assets			
Net assets			
Financed by:			
	Tracey	Matilda	Total

INTERPRET FINANCIAL STATEMENTS USING PROFITABILITY RATIOS

89 WHEELSTOGO

(a) Identify whether each of the following statements about profitability ratios is true or false.

	True ✓	False ✓
Ratio analysis is the only way to make conclusions about the financial performance or position of an entity		
Ratios are only useful if comparative information (i.e. prior year ratios, industry averages) is available		
Ratios give the users the ability to accurately determine the future performance of a business		

You are given the following information about a business, Wheelstogo:

Statement of profit or loss extract	£
Sales revenue	329,160
Gross profit	96,180
Profit for the year	65,350
Statement of financial position extract	£
Current liabilities	27,690
Non-current liabilities	34,600
Capital	106,200

(b) (i) Calculate the following ratios based upon the information above. Show your answers to two decimal places.

Return on capital employed (%)	
Gross profit margin (%)	

You have already calculated the selling expenses / revenue percentage for the current year as 14.8%.

The corresponding figure calculated from last year's accounts was 16%.

(b) (ii) Complete the following statement.

The selling expenses / revenue percentage shows …..PICKLIST…… when compared to the previous year's figures.

Picklist: an improvement, a deterioration

(c) **Identify what effect (if any) each of the following scenarios may have on the ratios stated.**

Each scenario is independent.

Scenario 1

Your company has managed to negotiate a lower price with a main supplier of your inventory. This has not affected the quality of goods you receive.

	Increase ✓	Unchanged ✓	Decrease ✓
Return on capital employed			
Gross profit percentage			

Scenario 2

The wage rates of administration staff have risen in line with others in the industry. The amount / skills level of the labour has been unaffected.

	Increase ✓	Unchanged ✓	Decrease ✓
Net profit percentage			
Cost of sales percentage			

90 PENTOP

(a) **Identify whether each of the following statements relating to profitability ratios is true or false.**

Statement	True ✓	False ✓
The interpretation of an entity's financial statements using ratios is only useful for existing shareholders.		
Return on capital employed is calculated as: gross profit/capital employed × 100		
A disadvantage of ratios is that they are based on previous performance which may not be valid for making predictions about the future.		
All other things being equal, if gross profit percentage increases, then the net profit percentage will decrease.		

You are given the following information about a business, Pentop:

Statement of profit or loss extract	£
Sales revenue	523,800
Gross profit	203,120
Total expenses	145,860
Profit for the year	57,260
Statement of financial position extract	£
Non-current assets	290,060
Current assets	46,790
Current liabilities	15,550
Non-current liabilities	87,500
Capital	142,400

(b) (i) **Calculate the following ratios based on the information above. Answers should be stated to two decimal places.**

Return on capital employed (%)	
Net profit margin (%)	

You have been advised that administration expenses as a percentage of revenue has increased in comparison with the previous year.

(b) (ii) **Identify whether each of the following statements about the increase in the ratio are true or false.**

Statement	True ✓	False ✓
The rise could have been caused by the business taking on a new employee within the accounts department.		
The rise could have been caused by revenue rising during the year due to increased advertising expenditure in the previous year.		

91 RUNPARK

(a)   Identify whether each of the following statements about profitability ratios is true or false.

Statement	True ✓	False ✓
The interpretation of an entity's financial statements using ratios is only useful for lenders.		
Achieving a gross profit margin of more than 5% is always considered an improvement in performance.		
A disadvantage of ratios is that they can be distorted through issues such as seasonality or creative accounting.		
Gross profit margin, net profit margin and return on capital employed must be disclosed on the face of the financial statements each year.		

You are given the following information about a business, Runpark:

Statement of profit or loss extract	£
Sales revenue	223,400
Gross profit	103,120
Total expenses	25,860
Profit for the year	77,260
Statement of financial position extract	£
Non-current assets	190,250
Current assets	36,970
Current liabilities	51,550
Non-current liabilities	47,500
Capital	196,400

(b)   (i)   Calculate the following ratios based on the information above. Answers should begiven to two decimal places.

Return on capital employed (%)	
Cost of sales / revenue ratio (%)	

Gross profit margin has risen compared to the previous year.

(ii) **Identify whether each of the following statements about the rise in the gross profit ratio are true or false.**

Statement	True ✓	False ✓
The rise in the ratio could have been caused by the successful launch of a new product with high demand creating an inflated launch price		
The rise in the ratio could have been due to savings in delivery fuel costs caused by reduced petrol prices.		

92 CRASHER

(a) **Identify whether each of the following statements about profitability ratios are true or false.**

	True ✓	False ✓
Return on capital employed is calculated using figures from both the statement of profit or loss and the statement of financial position.		
If a ratio reduces compared to the previous year, this will always mean that performance has deteriorated		
Ratios are the only way for users to analyse the performance of a business.		

You are given the following information about a business, Crasher.

Statement of profit or loss extract	£
Sales revenue	1,290,160
Gross profit	350.180
Net profit for the year	180,350
Statement of financial position extract	£
Non-current liabilities	534,600
Current liabilities	227,159
Capital	526,854

(b) **(i)** **Complete the following ratios based on the information above. Show your answers to two decimal places.**

Return on capital employed	
Net profit margin	

You have already calculated the gross profit percentage for the current year as 27.14%.

The corresponding figure calculated from last year's accounts was 24.65%.

(ii) **Complete the following statement.**

The gross profit percentage shows .....PICKLIST...... when compared to the previous year's figures.

PICKLIST
an improvement
a deterioration

(c) **Identify what effect (if any) each of the following scenarios may have on the ratios stated.**

Each scenario is independent.

Scenario 1

Your company has managed to negotiate a higher price per unit in a contract with a customer. There is no change in the sales volumes supplied in the contract or to the production process or associated costs.

	Increase ✓	Unchanged ✓	Decrease ✓
Cost of sales percentage			
Gross profit percentage			

Scenario 2

The wage rates of production staff have risen in line with others in the industry. The volume of outputs and skills level of the labour has been unaffected.

	Increase ✓	Unchanged ✓	Decrease ✓
Cost of sales percentage			
Gross profit percentage			

93 SHANNON

Shannon runs a building and construction business. Due to recent shortages, the cost of building materials has increased. Shannon has not attempted to pass the extra costs to her customers through price increases.

(a) **Identify whether each of the following statements is true or false.**

	True ✓	False ✓
Shannon's business' return on capital employed would increase		
Shannon's gross profit margin is likely to be unaffected		
Cost of sales/revenue percentage will increase		

You are given the following information about Shannon's business.

Statement of profit or loss extract	£
Sales revenue	469,750
Gross profit	146,580
Profit for the year	75,350
Statement of financial position extract	£
Total liabilities	54,600
Current liabilities	17,690
Capital	96,200

(b) (i) **Complete the following ratios based on the information above. Show your answers to two decimal places.**

Return on capital employed (%)

Gross profit margin (%)

Return on capital employed for the previous year was 40.65%.

(ii) **Complete the following statement.**

The return on capital employed shows .....PICKLIST...... when compared to the previous year's figures.

PICKLIST
an improvement
a deterioration

(c) **Identify what effect (if any) each of the following scenarios may have on the ratios and figures stated.**

Each scenario is independent.

Scenario 1

Your company has managed to negotiate a discount with a main supplier of your inventory. This has not affected the quality of goods you receive.

	Increase ✓	Unchanged ✓	Decrease ✓
Return on capital employed			
Revenue			

Scenario 2

A product has seen increased volumes of sales due to a large one-off advertising campaign in the year. Selling price structures and production processes and costs remained the same.

	Increase ✓	Unchanged ✓	Decrease ✓
Gross profit percentage			
Net profit percentage			

94   MAIZE

(a) **Identify whether each of the following statements about profitability ratios is true or false.**

Statement	True ✓	False ✓
Gross profit margins can only increase if sales prices have increased		
Capital employed is calculated as capital plus current liabilities		
Ratios can be used to compare the performance of different businesses in the same industry		
Ratios in isolation (e.g. without other ratios to provide a comparison) are not useful to the users of the financial statements		

You are given the following information about a business, Maize:

Statement of profit or loss extract	£
Sales revenue	421,226
Gross profit	153,128
Total expenses	100,860
Profit for the year	52,268

Statement of financial position extract	£
Non-current assets	290,125
Current assets	28,562
Current liabilities	31,850
Non-current liabilities	80,223
Capital	162,326

(b) (i) Calculate the following ratios based on the information above. Answers should be given to two decimal places.

Return on capital employed (%)

Net profit percentage (%)

Return on capital employed has risen compared to the previous year.

(c) Identify whether the following statements about the rise in the ratio are true or false.

Statement	True ✓	False ✓
A one-off advertising campaign that occurred in the previous year could have contributed to this increase.		
The performance of the entity has deteriorated		

95   PARKBENCH

(a)   **Identify whether each of the following statements about profitability ratios is true or false.**

	True ✓	False ✓
If the cost of production increases, gross profit margin would be expected to reduce		
All other things equal, increases in wages of the office and accounts staff would cause net profit margin to decrease		
Users know what is going to happen to a business going forward if they utilise ratio analysis of the business' financial information		

You are given the following information about a business, Parkbench:

Statement of profit or loss extract	£
Sales revenue	151,160
Gross profit	26,180
Profit for the year	16,350
Statement of financial position extract	£
Current liabilities	18,690
Non-current liabilities	25,600
Capital	16,200

(b)   (i)   **Complete the following ratios based on the information above. Show your answers to two decimal places.**

Return on capital employed (%)

Gross profit margin (%)

You have already calculated the selling expenses / revenue percentage for the current year as 82.68%. The corresponding figure calculated from last year's accounts was 72%.

(ii) Complete the following statement.

The selling expenses / revenue percentage shows …..PICKLIST…… when compared to the previous year's figures.

PICKLIST
an improvement
a deterioration

(c) Identify what effect (if any) each of the following scenarios may have on the ratios or figures stated.

Each scenario is independent.

Scenario 1

Your company has managed to negotiate a lower interest rate on its loans from the bank.

	Increase ✓	Unchanged ✓	Decrease ✓
Revenue			
Gross profit percentage			

Scenario 2

Due to competition in the market place, sales prices have been reduced with the aim of improving sales volumes. Production costs and other costs remain the same.

	Increase ✓	Unchanged ✓	Decrease ✓
Net profit percentage			
Cost of sales percentage			

PREPARE ACCOUNTING RECORDS FROM INCOMPLETE INFORMATION

96 MULTIPLE CHOICE QUESTIONS

1   The following information is available about a business:

Opening receivables	£54,550
Closing receivables	£52,560
Receipts from customers in the period	£98,460

Irrecoverable receivables written off during the period £2,000

Of the receipts from customers, £16,838 represented cash sales. What was the amount of sales on credit for the period?

A   £85,612

B   £79,632

C   £96,470

D   £81,632

2   The following information is available about the transactions of Razil, a sole trader who does not keep proper accounting records:

	£
Opening inventory	77,000
Closing inventory	84,000
Purchases	763,000
Gross profit margin	30%

Based on this information, what was Razil's sales revenue for the year?

A   £982,800

B   £1,090,000

C   £2,520,000

D   £1,080,000

3   On 1 September 20X8, Winston had inventory of £380,000. During the month, sales totalled £650,000 and purchases £480,000. On 30 September 20X8 a fire destroyed some of the inventory. The undamaged goods were valued at £220,000. The business makes all sales with a standard gross profit margin of 30%.

Based upon this information, what is the cost of the inventory destroyed in the fire?

A   £185,000

B   £140,000

C   £405,000

D   £360,000

4   During September, Edel had sales of £148,000, which made a gross profit of £40,000. Purchases amounted to £100,000 and opening inventory was £34,000.

What was the value of closing inventory?

A   £24,000

B   £26,000

C   £42,000

D   £54,000

5   **Which of the following gives a gross profit mark-up of 40%?**

A   Sales are £120,000 and gross profit is £48,000

B   Sales are £120,000 and cost of sales is £72,000

C   Sales are £100,800 and cost of sales is £72,000

D   Sales are £100,800 and cost of sales is £60,480

97   A CATERING BUSINESS

You are working on the financial statements of a catering business for the year ended 31 May 20X3. You have the following information:

Day book summaries:	Goods £	VAT £	Total £
Sales	241,000	48,200	289,200
Purchases	94,000	18,800	112,800

Balances as at:	31 May X2 £	31 May X3 £
Trade receivables	26,000	12,000
Trade payables	21,500	16,800

Further information:	Net £	VAT £	Total £
Office expenses	8,000	1,600	9,600
Office expenses are not included in the purchases day book			

Bank summary	Dr £		Cr £
Balance b/d	9,620	Travel expenses	14,000
Trade receivables	294,878	Office expenses	9,600
Interest received	102	Trade payables	115,150
Cash sales (inc VAT)	18,000	HMRC for VAT	27,525
		Drawings	101,000
		Payroll expenses	10,000
		Balance c/d	45,325
	322,600		322,600

(a)   Using the figures given above, prepare the receivables control account for the year ended 31 May 20X3. Show clearly discounts as the balancing figure.

Receivables control account

(b)   Find the closing balance for VAT by preparing the VAT control account for the year ended 31 May 20X3. Use the figures given above.

Note: The business is not charged VAT on its travel expenses.

VAT control

		Balance b/d	4,300

98 LOCKE TRADING

You are working on the financial statements of Locke Trading for the year ended 30 September 20X9. You have the following information:

Day book summaries:	Goods £	VAT £	Total £
Sales	195,000	39,000	234,000
Purchases	93,600	18,720	112,320

Balances as at:	30 Sep X8 £	30 Sep X9 £
Trade receivables	16,500	20,625
Trade payables	8,700	12,130

Further information:	Net £	VAT £	Total £
Admin expenses	37,000	7,400	44,400
Office expenses	6,500	1,300	7,800
Admin and office expenses are not included in the purchases day book			

Bank summary	Dr £		Cr £
Balance b/d	8,725	Travel expenses	4,650
Trade receivables	225,000	Office expenses	7,800
Interest received	79	Trade payables	105,204
		Admin expenses	44,400
		Rent	1,500
		HMRC for VAT	6,450
		Drawings	25,000
		Payroll expenses	13,600
		Balance c/d	25,200
	233,804		233,804

You have been advised that you need to account for a contra amount of £500 which has been offset against amounts due between Locke Trading and another business which makes both purchases and sales on credit to Locke Trading.

(a) **Using the figures given above, prepare the payables ledger control account for the year ended 30 September 20X9. Show clearly discounts as the balancing figure.**

Payables ledger control account

(b) **Using the figures above find the closing balance for VAT by preparing the VAT control account for the year ended 30 September 20X9.**

VAT control

		Balance b/d	2,300

99   FIRST POSITION BALLET SUPPLIES

You are working on the financial statements of a business called First Position Ballet Supplies for the year ended 31 December 20X2. You have the following information:

Day book summaries:	Goods £	VAT £	Total £
Sales	105,000	21,000	126,000
Purchases	92,000	18,400	110,400

Balances as at:	31 Dec X1 £	31 Dec X2 £
Trade receivables	8,100	11,500
Trade payables	12,400	9,800
Prepayment	300	450
Accrual	250	?

Returns day book summaries:	Net £	VAT £	Total £
Sales	19,000	3,800	22,800
Purchases	8,000	1,600	9,600

Bank summary	Dr £		Cr £
Balance b/d	23,400	Electricity expense	5,000
Trade receivables	96,590	Trade payables	?
Interest received	3,810	HMRC	6,100
		Rent	10,000
		Balance c/d	4,200
	123,800		123,800

(a)   What is the amount paid through the bank account to trade payables in the year?

£_____

(b) Using the figures given above (including your answer to part (a), prepare the payables ledger control account for the year ended 31 December 20X2, showing clearly discounts received as the balancing figure.

Payables ledger control account

(c) The prepayment shown in the schedule is for rent.

Using the figures above, calculate the charge to the statement of profit or loss for the year.

Rent expense

(d) The accrual shown above is for electricity.

If the electricity charge to the statement of profit or loss for the year is £5,125, calculate the closing accrual.

Electricity expense

100 RELIABLE CARS

You are working on the accounts of Reliable Cars for the year ended 30 September 20X6. You have the following information:

Sales for the year ended 30 September 20X6

- Credit sales amounted to £46,000 net of VAT
- Cash sales amounted to £212,000 net of VAT
- All sales are standard rated for VAT at 20%.

Payments from the bank account for the year ended 30 September 20X6

- Payroll expenses   £48,000
- Administration expenses   £6,400 ignore VAT
- Vehicle running costs   £192,000 including VAT at 20%
- Drawings   £41,800
- VAT   £17,300

Summary of balances available

Balance as at	30 September 20X5	30 September 20X6
Bank account	5,630	8,140
Trade receivables	4,120	5,710
VAT (credit balances)	4,200	4,575

(a) Calculate the figure for credit sales for entry into the receivables ledger control account?

£_____

(b) Using the figures given above (including your answer to part (a), prepare the receivables ledger control account for the year ended 30 September 20X6, showing clearly the receipts paid into the bank as the balancing figure.

Receivables ledger control account

(c) Calculate the cash sales inclusive of VAT which have been paid into the bank account. All cash sales are banked.

£_____

(d) **Show a summarised bank account for the year ended 30 September 20X6.**

Bank account

101 I.T. SOLUTIONS

I.T. Solutions is owned by Justin Long and started trading on 1 October 20X8. You have been provided with the following summarised bank account, and are required to assist in the preparation of the first set of accounts for the year ended 30 September 20X9.

Bank summary for the year ended 30 September 20X9

Capital introduced	16,000	Rent of premises	8,000
Receipts from trade receivables	49,600	Payments to trade payables	18,160
		Travel expenses	4,300
		Administration expenses	3,270
		Drawings	28,000
		Balance c/d	3,870
	65,600		65,600

Additional information:

- Justin transferred his own vehicle into the business on 1 October 20X8. It was valued at £4,000.

- On 30 September 20X9, trade receivables owed £6,300.

- On 30 September 20X9, trade payables were owed £2,500. Total supplies during the year were £22,000.

(a)   Prepare the receivables ledger control account showing clearly the credit sales as the balancing figure.

Receivables ledger control account

(b)   Prepare the payables ledger control account showing clearly the discounts received as the balancing figure.

Payables ledger control account

(c)   Prepare the opening capital account as at 1 October 20X8, showing clearly all the capital introduced.

Capital account

102 BYRNE

You are working on the financial statements of Byrne who runs a clothing business for the year ended 31 May 20X6. You have the following information:

Day book summaries:	Goods £	VAT £	Total £
Sales	270,000	54,000	324,000
Purchases	180,000	36,000	216,000

Balances as at:	31 May X5 £	31 May X6 £
Trade receivables	28,500	24,000
Trade payables	23,750	19,600

Further information:	Net £	VAT £	Total £
Office expenses	9,500	1,900	11,400
Office expenses are not included in the purchases day book			

Bank summary	Dr £		Cr £
Trade receivables	324,996	Balance b/d	1,756
Interest received	150	Travel expenses	13,600
Cash sales (inc VAT)	36,000	Office expenses	11,400
		Trade payables	220,150
		HMRC for VAT	26,715
		Drawings	45,000
		Payroll expenses	25,000
		Balance c/d	17,525
	361,146		361,146

(a) **Using the figures given above, prepare the receivables ledger control account for the year ended 31 May 20X6. Show clearly sales returns as the balancing figure.**

Receivables ledger control account

(b) Using the figures given above, prepare the payables ledger control account for the year ended 31 May 20X6.

Payables ledger control account

(c) Find the closing balance for VAT by preparing the VAT control account for the year ended 31 May 20X6. Use the figures given above.

Note: The business is not charged VAT on its travel expenses.

		Balance b/d	8,300

103 PERCY

You are given the following information about a sole trader called Percy as at 31 March 20X2:

The value of assets and liabilities were:

- Non-current assets at carrying amount £14,000
- Bank £2,500
- Trade payables £10,300
- Opening capital (at 1 April 20X1) £3,700
- Drawings for the year £1,500

There were no other assets or liabilities.

(a) Calculate the profit for the year ended 30 March 20X2.

£_____

(b) **Tick the boxes to show whether increases to the account balances would be a debit or credit.**

You must choose ONE answer for EACH balance.

	Debit	**Credit**
Sales		
Prepayment		
Loan		
Accrual		
Trade receivables		

104 GROVER

You are given the following information about a sole trader called Grover as at 1 April 20X8:

The value of assets and liabilities were:

• Non-current assets at carrying amount	£17,150
• Trade receivables	£4,600
• Allowance for doubtful receivables	£350
• Prepayments	£200
• Bank overdraft	£600
• Trade payables	£3,750
• Accruals	£325
• Capital	£11,475

There were no other assets or liabilities, with the exception of part (a)

(a) **Calculate the long term loan account balance as at 1 April 20X8.**

£_____

(b) **Calculate the accumulated depreciation as at 1 April 20X8 if the non-current asset cost is £75,000.**

£_____

(c) On 1 June 20X8 a piece of equipment is disposed of and the proceeds received by cheque.

Tick the boxes to show what effect this transaction will have on the balances. You must choose ONE answer for EACH line.

	Debit	**Credit**	**No change**
Non-current assets cost			
Accumulated depreciation			
Trade receivables			
Trade payables			
Bank			

105 CHIRON

You are given the following information about a sole trader called Chiron as at 31 January 20X5:

The value of assets and liabilities were:

• Non-current assets at cost	£10,000
• Trade receivables	£2,000
• Loan	£7,500
• Closing capital (at 31 January 20X5)	£3,500

There were no other assets or liabilities.

(a) **Calculate the amount of accumulated depreciation at the year end 31 January 20X5**

£_____

(b) **Chiron sells goods at a mark-up of 25%. What would be the gross profit on a sales price of £11,000?**

£_____

106 PARKER

You are given the following information about the business of Parker, a sole trader, as at 1 April 20X8:

The value of assets and liabilities were:

• Non-current assets at cost	£25,725
• Non-current asset accumulated depreciation	£8,670
• Trade receivables after allowance for doubtful receivables	£4,790
• Prepayments	£190
• Long-term loan	£7,410
• Trade payables	£4,250
• Accruals	£360
• Capital	£10,130

There were no other assets or liabilities, with the exception of part (a)

(a) **Calculate the bank balance as at 1 April 20X8.**

£_____

(b) **Calculate the trade receivables figure as at 1 April 20X8 if the allowance for doubtful receivables is £480.**

£_____

(c)   On 1 June 20X8 a piece of equipment is disposed of and the proceeds received in cash.

Tick the boxes to show what effect this transaction will have on the balances. You must choose ONE answer for EACH line.

	Debit	Credit	No change
Non-current assets cost			
Accumulated depreciation			
Trade receivables			
Bank balance			
Cash balance			

107   ANNABETH

You are given the following information about a sole trader called Annabeth as at 30 September:

The following balances are available:

Assets and liabilities as at:	30 Sept 20X3 £
Plant and equipment at cost	19,000
Plant and equipment accumulated depreciation	5,600
Inventory at cost	2,890
Cash	560
Bank	2,310
Prepayment for rent	550
Payables for materials	1,720
Accrual for travel expenses	380

Calculate the figure for capital as at 30 September 2003.

£_____

108 RUBICON

You make an entry for two transactions in a sole trader's accounts.

The table below shows the total assets and liabilities before and after the transactions:

Balances:	Before £	After £
Total assets	42,135	43,385
Total liabilities	28,653	29,273

Calculate the amount by which the capital balance has changed as a result of the transactions.

£_____

109 LUKE

Luke sells office equipment. He buys a photocopier for £900.

(a) **What would the selling price be, excluding VAT, if a 40% mark-up was applied?**

(b) **What would the selling price be, excluding VAT, if the sales margin was 40%?**

110 MARK UPPS AND MARGE INNS

Mark Upps and Marge Inns sell kitchen equipment and fittings.

(a) **If they buy a gas cooker for £825 excluding VAT, what would the selling price be, excluding VAT, if a 40% mark-up was applied?**

£_____

(b) **If they buy a gas cooker for £825 excluding VAT, what would the selling price be, excluding VAT, if the sales margin was 40%?**

£_____

(c) **If they buy a freezer for £250 excluding VAT, what would the profit be, excluding VAT, if a 20% mark-up was applied?**

£_____

(d) **If they buy a freezer for £250 excluding VAT, what would the profit be, excluding VAT, if the sales margin was 20%?**

£_____

(e) **If they sell a dishwasher for £455 excluding VAT, what would the purchase price be, excluding VAT, if a 30% mark-up was included in the selling price?**

£_____

(f) **If they sell a dishwasher for £455 excluding VAT, what would the purchase price be, excluding VAT, if a 30% sales margin was included in the selling price?**

£_____

Section 2

ANSWERS TO PRACTICE QUESTIONS

UNDERSTAND THE ACCOUNTING PRINCIPLES UNDERLYING FINAL ACCOUNTS PREPARATION

1   MULTIPLE CHOICE QUESTIONS

    1   C

    2   D

    3   C

    4   B

    5   B

    6   C

    7   C

    8   C

    9   C

   10   C

2   USERS OF THE FINAL ACCOUNTS

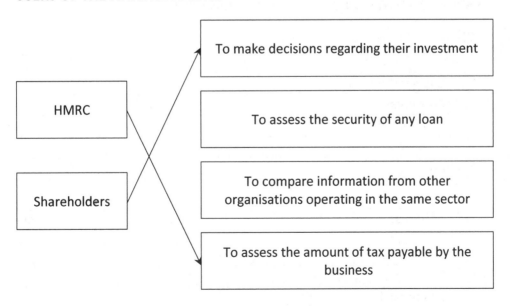

3 THE FUNDAMENTAL QUALITATIVE CHARACTERISTICS

	✓
Faithful representation	✓
Objectivity	
Communication	
Relevance	✓
Comparability	
Understandability	

4 BORIS

	✓
Accruals	
Going concern	✓
Consistency	
None of the above	

Going concern is particularly relevant here because there is doubt over whether the business will continue trading for the foreseeable future.

5 INTERNATIONAL ACCOUNTING STANDARDS

	IAS 2 ✓	IAS 16 ✓
Property, plant and equipment is measured at its cost and depreciated so that its depreciable amount is allocated over its useful life.		✓
Inventories should be valued at the lower of cost and net realisable value.	✓	

6 USERS AND QUALITIES OF FINANCIAL INFORMATION

(a)   (i)

	✓
Current shareholders	✓
Customers	
Government	
Competitors	
Lenders	✓

(ii)

Definition	Fundamental ✓	Enhancing ✓
Verifiability		✓
Relevance	✓	
Comparability		✓
Faithful representation	✓	

7   ACCOUNTING PRINCIPLES AND CHARACTERISTICS I

(a)   (i)

Scenario	Principle
The business recognises the costs of using a broadband connection during the period despite having not been billed by the network provider.	Accruals principle
Jiaoming owns and runs a gym and takes a set of dumbbells home for own use. This is recorded as drawings.	Business entity principle
Stationery items such as staplers are treated as expenses rather than as non-current assets.	Materiality principle
The business presents non-current assets and non-current liabilities separately In the statement of financial position.	Going concern principle

(ii)

Definition	Term
When knowledgeable and independent observers reach a consensus that the information presented is faithfully represented.	Verifiability
Providing information to decision makers at a point that will make it capable of influencing their economic decisions.	Timeliness

8   ACCOUNTING PRINCIPLES AND CHARACTERISTICS II

(a)   (i)

Scenario	Principle
Accounting policies should not be changed regularly from one year to the next, unless the change provides a more true and fair view.	Consistency
Income received in advance is recorded as deferred income in the statement of financial position until the service is provided at a future date, at which point the income is recorded in the statement of profit or loss.	Accruals
The owners of a business take a mobile phone from their business' supplies to give to their daughter for her birthday and record this as drawings	Business entity principle
The business presents non-current assets and non-current liabilities separately in the statement of financial position.	Going concern principle

(ii)

Scenario	Qualitative characteristic
Providing information that is complete, neutral and free from error.	Faithful representation
Classifying, characterising and presenting information clearly and concisely.	Understandability

9 ACCOUNTING PRINCIPLES I

(a) (i)

	✓
Verifiability	
Accruals	
Faithful representation	✓
Going concern	
Relevance	✓

(a) (ii)

Definition	Accounting principle
Sales revenue should be recognised when goods and services have been supplied; costs are incurred when goods and services have been received	Accruals
Financial statements are produced using the assumption that a business will remain in business for the foreseeable future.	Going concern
Transactions and valuation methods are treated the same way from year to year. This means that users of accounts can, therefore, make more meaningful comparisons of financial performance from year to year.	Consistency
Expenses are included in the accounts as soon as there is a reasonable chance that such costs will be incurred in the future.	Prudence

10 FINANCIAL STATEMENTS

(a) **(i)** The financial statements are produced by the directors so that the users can assess the financial performance of the business

(ii)

Definition	Accounting concept or qualitative characteristic
Understandability	Qualitative characteristic
Relevance	Qualitative characteristic
Going Concern	Accounting concept
Accruals	Accounting concept

11 ACCOUNTING PRINCIPLES II

(a) **(i)**

Scenario	Principle
From one year to the next, a business uses the same approach to calculate its depreciation and its allowance for doubtful receivables	Consistency principle
A business records an allowance for doubtful receivables against its receivables despite there still being a chance of receiving the outstanding amount	Prudence
A payment made to a supplier for services that will be received in the next accounting period will be recorded as a prepayment	Accruals
Capital purchases with a value lower than a certain threshold set by the owners can be written off directly to the profit or loss as an expense	Materiality

(ii)

Statement	True ✓	False ✓
Relevance is an enhancing qualitative characteristic of useful financial information		✓
The lenders of a business are considered one of the primary users of the financial statements	✓	

12   USERS OF FINAL ACCOUNTS

(a)   (i)

	✓
Current shareholders	✓
Customers	
Lenders	✓
Competitors	
Management	

(a)   (ii)

Definition	Fundamental or enhancing
Verifiability	Enhancing
Faithful representation	Fundamental
Comparability	Enhancing
Understandability	Enhancing

UNDERSTAND THE PRINCIPLES OF ADVANCED DOUBLE-ENTRY BOOKKEEPING

13   MULTIPLE CHOICE QUESTIONS

1   **C**

An increase in capital and an increase in liability both require credit entries in the appropriate accounts. Debits and credits must match each other.

2   **D**

The accounting equation is Assets = Capital + Liabilities.

So, we can have: Assets (£14,000) = Capital (£10,000) + Liabilities (£4,000)

3   **C**

Electricity is an expense. Assets and expenses accounts have debit balances. The remainder are examples of income and liabilities which have credit balances.

4   **D**

Trade payables are short-term liabilities. All liabilities have credit balances. The other items are drawings, an expense and an asset, all of which have debit balances.

5   **C**

The separate entity principle relates to the business and its owner. Separate entity recognises the difference between them. A and B focus on different aspects of the accounts but are within the business. There is a clear separation between owner of a business and a lender.

6   **C**

A bank overdraft is a liability as technically it is repayable whenever the bank demands. Accounts receivables and inventories are assets, and drawings represent a withdrawal of capital.

7   **A**

Petty cash, the salesman's motor car and computer software are all examples of assets. The owner is a liability representing the amount the business owes its owner.

14   DOUBLE-ENTRY

(a)   A sole trader makes a credit sale (ignore VAT)

	Debit	Credit	No change
Revenue		✓	
Loan			✓
Non-current assets			✓
Trade receivables	✓		

(b)   A sole trader decides to write off an irrecoverable debt

	Debit	Credit	No change
Trade payables			✓
Inventory			✓
Irrecoverable debt expense	✓		
Trade receivables		✓	

(c)   A sole trader purchases a new computer on credit for use in the business

	Debit	Credit	No change
Discount allowed			✓
Sundry payables		✓	
Non-current assets	✓		
Inventory			✓

(d) A sole trader accounts for the cash received on disposal of a motor vehicle

	Debit	Credit	No change
Motor vehicles repairs			✓
Motor vehicles depreciation expense			✓
Disposal of motor vehicles account		✓	
Bank	✓		

(e) A sole trader pays transport costs to have goods delivered to the premises of the business

	Debit	Credit	No change
Bank		✓	
Carriage inwards	✓		
Carriage outwards			✓
Purchases			✓

(f) A sole trader pays transport costs to have goods delivered to customers

	Debit	Credit	No change
Bank		✓	
Carriage inwards			✓
Carriage outwards	✓		
Sales			✓

15 CLASSIFYING TRANSACTIONS AND BALANCES

(a) Asset – inventory

(b) Expense

(c) Income

(d) Asset – trade receivables

(e) Expense

(f) Liability (this is a special liability known as capital)

(g) Liability – payables

(h) Asset

(i) Asset

(j) Income

(k) Asset

16   BILL SMITH – ACCOUNTING EQUATION

(a)   Bill Smith starts a new business by putting £10,000 into a business bank account.

Assets =	Capital	+ Profit	– Drawings	+ Liabilities
10,000	10,000			

(b)   A bank lends the business a further £5,000.

Assets =	Capital	+ Profit	– Drawings	+ Liabilities
15,000	10,000			5,000

(c)   Bill buys a delivery van for £6,000.

Assets =	Capital	+ Profit	– Drawings	+ Liabilities
15,000	10,000			5,000

Although the accounting equation looks the same as in (b) above, the assets now consist of cash at bank (£9,000) and van (£6,000).

(d)   Bill buys inventory for £2,500 by writing out a business cheque.

Assets =	Capital	+ Profit	– Drawings	+ Liabilities
15,000	10,000			5,000

Although the accounting equation looks the same as in (b) above, the assets now consist of cash at bank (£6,500), inventory (£2,500) and van (£6,000).

(e)   All the inventory is sold for £4,000. The money is paid direct to the business bank account.

Step 1   Work out profit

	£
Sales	4,000
Cost of sales	2,500
	————
Profit	1,500
	————

Step 2   Insert into accounting equation

Assets =	Capital	+ Profit	– Drawings	+ Liabilities
16,500	10,000	1,500		5,000

The assets now consist of cash at bank (£10,500) and van (£6,000).

Conclusion

Remember that all of the £4,000 sales proceeds is paid into the bank account.

(f)   Bill pays a business expense of £400 out of the business bank account.

Step 1 Work out new profit

	£
Sales	4,000
Expenses	
Cost of sales	(2,500)
Sundry expenses	(400)
Profit	1,100

Step 2 Insert into accounting equation

Assets =	Capital	+ Profit	− Drawings	+ Liabilities
16,100	10,000	1,100		5,000

The assets now consist of cash at bank (£10,100) and van (£6,000).

(g)   Finally Bill takes £300 out of the business for his own purposes.

Assets =	Capital	+ Profit	− Drawings	+ Liabilities
15,800	10,000	1,100	(300)	5,000

Cash at bank is now reduced to £9,800. The other remaining asset is the van (£6,000).

17   ASSETS OR LIABILITIES?

(a)   Asset

(b)   Asset

(c)   Liability

(d)   Asset

(e)   Liability

(f)   Asset

(g)   Asset

18   TERMINOLOGY

(a)   An **asset** is a present resource controlled by the **entity** as a result of a past **event**.

(b)   A **liability** is an amount owed by the business to another business or individual.

Examples include a **loan from a bank** and amounts owed to the suppliers of goods or services which have yet to be paid for – payables.

(c)   **Inventory** is an asset comprising goods purchased for resale, components for inclusion in manufactured products, and the finished products which have been manufactured which have not yet been sold.

(d)   **Capital** is the liability of the business to the owner of the business.

(e)   **Drawings** is the term which refers to amounts taken out of the business by the owner.

19   ALI

£3,150

Bank

	£		£
Balance b/f	1,780	Drawings (4 × £200)	800
Receipt after trade discount	570		
Receipt from customer	400		
Bankings from canteen receipts	1,200	Balance c/f	3,150
	3,950		3,950

Trade discounts are deducted at source by the seller and only the reduced amount will be payable by the customer. Therefore, the net amount of £570 must have been received during the month.

20   MIN

Task 1

State the accounting entries required to record the return of goods to the supplier.	£000	Credit/Debit
Revenue		
Returns inwards		
Returns outwards (100/120 × £300)	250	Credit
VAT (20/120 × £300)	50	Credit
Trade payables' ledger control account	300	Debit
Trade receivables' ledger control account		

Task 2

	£000	Credit/Debit
Drawings	15	Debit
Trade payables' ledger control account		
Purchases	15	Credit
Revenue		

ACCOUNTING FOR AND MONITORING NON-CURRENT ASSETS

21 MULTIPLE CHOICE QUESTIONS

1   **D**

2   **A**

The difference between the two records is £10,000. The disposed asset must have had a carrying amount of this amount.

3   **D**

4   **C**

	Ledger Account:	£
Debit	Depreciation expense account	3,500
Credit	Accumulated depreciation account – buildings	3,500

5   **D**

A non-current asset register is a detailed schedule of non-current assets, and is not another name for non-current asset ledger accounts in the general ledger.

6   **B**

	£	£	£
Year 1 Cost less dep'n @ 20%	2,400.00	(480.00)	1,920.00
Year 2 Dep'n (20% × £1,920)		(384.00)	1,536.00
Year 3 Dep'n (20% × £1,536)		(307.20)	1,228.80
Year 4 Sale proceeds			1,200.00
Loss on disposal			(28.80)

7   £86,000

	£
Purchase cost of machine	80,000
Installation	5,000
Pre-production safety testing	1,000
	86,000

A non-current asset should be measured initially at its cost. 'Cost' means the amounts incurred to acquire the asset and bring it into working condition for its intended use. These include the purchase cost, initial delivery and handling costs, installation costs and professional fees. Costs of testing whether the asset is working properly may be included, but staff training costs cannot be capitalised.

8   **A**

		£
Cost		5,000
	Year 1 (20% × 5,000)	(1,000)
	Year 2 (20% × 4,000)	(800)
	Year 3 (20% × 3,200)	(640)
Carrying amount at time of disposal		2,560
Sale proceeds		2,200
Loss on disposal		360

9   **D**

Painting and replacing windows are maintenance and repairs, and so are classified as an expense and must be taken to the statement of profit or loss. The purchase of a car for resale means that the car is an item of inventory for the business, not a non-current asset. Legal fees incurred in purchasing a building are included in the cost of the building, and so are part of the non-current asset cost, i.e. asset expenditure.

10   **D**

Disposals account

	£		£
Cost	12,000	Accumulated depreciation	7,200
		(3 years × 20% × £12,000)	
Profit (β)	200	Proceeds (part-exchange allowance)	5,000
	12,200		12,200

22   SOUTHGATE TRADING

Description	Acquisition date	Cost £	Depreciation charges £		Carrying amount £	Funding method	Disposal proceeds	Disposal date
Computer equipment								
Server main office	30/09/X6	2,800.00				Cash		
Year end 31/03/X7			840.00		1,960.00			
Year end 31/03/X8			840.00		1,120.00			
Year end 31/03/X9			**840.00**		**280.00**			
HP printer 65438LKR	**28/03/X9**	**775.00**				**Credit**		
Year end 31/03/X9			**232.50**		**542.50**			
Motor vehicles								
AB08 DRF	01/04/X6	12,000.00				Cash		
Year end 31/03/X7			3,000.00		9,000.00			
Year end 31/03/X8			2,250.00		6,750.00			
Year end 31/03/X9			0		0		4,500.00	15/03/X9
AB 07 FRP	31/01/X8	9,600.00				Cash		
Year end 31/03/X8			2,400.00		7,200.00			
Year end 31/03/X9			**1,800.00**		**5,400.00**			

(d)   £660 (£250 + £410) – the cost of repainting the office is considered to be maintenance – revenue expenditure.

23   TK FABRICATIONS

Description	Acquisition date	Cost £	Depreciation charges £	Carrying amount £	Funding method	Disposal proceeds	Disposal date
Equipment							
Workshop fit out	17/07/X6	5,400.00			Cash		
Year end 31/01/X7			810.00	4,590.00			
Year end 31/01/X8			810.00	3,780.00			
Year end 31/01/X9			810.00	2,970.00			
Welding iron 289XP4	**28/01/X9**	**865.00**			**Credit**		
Year end 31/01/X9			**129.75**	**735.25**			
Motor vehicles							
PF07 THY	04/06/X6	13,500.00			Cash		
Year end 31/01/X7			3,375.00	10,125.00			
Year end 31/01/X8			2,531.25	7,593.75			
Year end 31/01/X9			0	0		**8,500.00**	**20/01/X9**
SR08 EKE	24/01/X8	7,300.00			Part-exchange		
Year end 31/01/X8			1,825.00	5,475.00			
Year end 31/01/X9			**1,368.75**	**4,106.25**			

24   BYTES TECHNOLOGY GROUP

Description	Acquisition date	Cost £	Depreciation charges £	Carrying amount £	Funding method	Disposal proceeds	Disposal date
Computer equipment							
Mainframe Server	17/07/X6	14,000.00			Cash		
Year end 31/03/X7			2,800.00	11,200.00			
Year end 31/03/X8			2,800.00	8,400.00			
Year end 31/03/X9			**2,800.00**	**5,600.00**			
Printer 180G92	**28/03/X9**	**560.00**			**Credit**		
Year end 31/03/X9			**112.00**	**448.00**			
Motor vehicles							
EJ09 TYZ	14/09/X6	9,000.00			Cash		
Year end 31/03/X7			2,700.00	6,300.00			
Year end 31/03/X8			1,890.00	4,410.00			
Year end 31/03/X9			0	0		**3,200.00**	**20/03/X9**
EA55 SAR	12/02/X8	10,000.00			Part-exchange		
Year end 31/03/X8			3,000.00	7,000.00			
Year end 31/03/X9			**2,100.00**	**4,900.00**			

(d)

	Tick
The location of the asset	✓

25   JACO TRADING

Extract from the non-current assets register

Description	Acquisition date	Cost £	Depreciation charges £	Carrying amount £	Funding method	Disposal proceeds	Disposal date
Kitchen equipment							
American-style fridge freezer	01/04/X5	2,000.00			Cash		
Year end 31/03/X6			500.00	1,500.00			
Year end 31/03/X7			375.00	1,125.00			
Year end 31/03/X8			**281.25**	**843.75**			
Electric deck pizza oven	**01/04/X7**	**3,765.00**			**Lease**		
Year end 31/03/X8			**941.25**	**2,823.75**			
Computer equipment							
Desktop 132	01/10/X5	1,220.00			Cash		
Year end 31/03/X6			122.00	1,098.00			
Year end 31/03/X7			244.00	854.00			
Year end 31/03/X8			**244.00**	**610.00**			
Laptop 4911	01/01/X6	1,000.00			Cash		
Year end 31/03/X6			50.00	950.00			
Year end 31/03/X7			200.00	750.00			
Year end 31/03/X8			**100.00**	**0.00**		**200.00**	**30/09/X7**

26 VIVIENNE

Disposals

Computer equipment – cost	4,000	Computer equipment – accumulated depreciation	3,200
Statement of profit or loss	200	Computer equipment – cost	1,000
	4,200		4,200

Bank

Balance b/d	10,761	Computer equipment – cost	4,000
		Balance c/d	6,761
	10,761		10,761

27 A PARTNERSHIP

Vehicles at cost

Balance b/d	10,000	Balance c/d	17,500
Bank	7,500		
	17,500		17,500

Vehicles accumulated depreciation

Balance c/d	4,500	Balance b/d	3,000
		Depreciation charge	1,500
	4,500		4,500

Depreciation charge

Balance b/d	1,000	Statement of profit or loss	2,500
Vehicles accumulated depreciation	1,500		
	2,500		2,500

	Tick
A partner of the business	✓

28   SOLE TRADER

Vehicles at cost

Balance b/d	26,000	Balance c/d	**44,000**
Bank	18,000		
	44,000		44,000

Vehicles accumulated depreciation

Balance c/d	**8,800**	Balance b/d	6,500
		Depreciation charge	**2,300**
	8,800		8,800

Depreciation charge

Balance b/d	3,000	**Statement of profit or loss**	**5,300**
Vehicles accumulated depreciation	2,300		
	5,300		5,300

29   KATY'S CAKES

Equipment at cost

Balance b/d	6,200	**Balance c/d**	**14,700**
Bank	8,500		
	14,700		14,700

Equipment accumulated depreciation

Balance c/d	**3,180**	Balance b/d	1,900
		Depreciation charge – existing	**430**
		Depreciation charge – new	**850**
	3,180		3,180

Depreciation charge

Balance b/d	3,000	**Statement of profit or loss**	**4,280**
Accum. Dep'n – existing	430		
Accum. Dep'n – new	850		
	4,280		4,280

(d)

	✓
The money put in by the owners of the business	
The money spent on the purchase of non-current assets	✓
The total amount of capital owed to the owner of the business	

30   MILES 2 GO

Narrative	Dr	Cr
Disposals	12,000.00	
Vehicles at cost		12,000.00
Vehicles accumulated depreciation	9,119.00	
Disposals		9,119.00
Vehicles at cost	15,250.00	
Motor vehicle expenses	210.00	
Disposals		3,800.00
Sundry payables		11,660.00
Totals	36,579.00	36,579.00

31   FLINT FARMS

(a)

Narrative	Dr	Cr
Disposals	32,000.00	
Vehicle at cost		32,000.00
Vehicles accumulated depreciation*	8,672.00	
Disposals		8,672.00
Vehicle at cost	40,800.00	
Insurance	2,500.00	
Disposals		8,500.00
Sundry payables		34,800.00
Totals	83,972.00	83,972.00

Key answer tips

The length of ownership of this vehicle is 2 years 11 months; therefore it was acquired on 18th September W7. The year end is 30th September and a full year's depreciation is charged in the year of acquisition with no charge in the year of disposal. This vehicle will be depreciated for year W7, W8 & W9 (it is disposed of in X0 therefore in accordance with the policy no depreciation will be charged in this year). Therefore, three years of depreciation are charged at 10% diminishing-balance basis.

Year W7 £32,000 × 10% = £3,200

Year W8 £28,800 × 10% = £2,880

Year W9 £25,920 × 10% = £2,592

Accumulated depreciation £8,672

(b)

Rent	Revenue
Van	Capital
Installation of air conditioning	Capital
Repairing a window	Revenue

32 LEO LIGHTING

(a)   Year ended 31/12/X1 £20,000 × 10% = £2,000

   Year ended 31/12/X2 (£20,000 – £2,000) × 10% = £1,800

   Year ended 31/12/X3 (£20,000 – £2,000 – £1,800) × 10% = £1,620

   Total accumulated depreciation (£2,000 + £1,800 + £1,620) = £5,420

(b)

Narrative	Dr	Cr
Disposals account	20,000	
Machinery cost account		20,000
Machinery accumulated depreciation account	5,420	
Disposals account		5,420
Bank	10,000	
VAT Control (20/120 × £10,000)		1,667
Disposals account (100/120 × £10,000)		8,333
Totals	35,420	35,420

Disposals

Machinery at cost	20,000	Machinery accumulated depreciation	5,420
		Bank	8,333
		Loss on disposal	6,247
	20,000		20,000

The profit or loss on disposal can also be calculated by comparing the sales proceeds to the carrying amount. The sales proceeds are £8,333 compared to a carrying amount of £14,580.

Therefore, a loss of £6,247 has been made.

33 FRED FARRIER

(a)   £1,600

  (£9,250 – £1,250)/5 years

(b) & (c)

Equipment at cost

Balance b/d	38,200		
Bank	9,250		
		Balance c/d	47,450
	47,450		47,450

Equipment accumulated depreciation

		Balance b/d	12,200
		Depreciation charges	1,600
Balance c/d	13,800		
	13,800		13,800

Depreciation charge

Balance b/d	2,300		
Accumulated depreciation (equipment)	1,600		
		Statement of profit or loss	3,900
	3,900		3,900

(d)   £5,500

(e)   £512

Tutorial note

The carrying amount is calculated by deducting the accumulated depreciation from the cost.

Cost – accumulated depreciation = carrying amount

Calculation of accumulated depreciation:

Depreciation charges for years 1 – 3

Year 1: £1,000 × 20%	£200
Year 2: (£1,000 – £200) × 20%	£160
Year 3: (£1,000 – £200 – £160) × 20%	£128
	———
Accumulated depreciation	£488

Carrying amount = £512 (cost £1,000 – accumulated depreciation £488)

RECORD PERIOD END ADJUSTMENTS

34   MULTIPLE CHOICE QUESTIONS

1   **A**

2   **B**

3   **C**

4   **B**

5   **C**

6   **C**

The year to 31 December 20X3 includes 9 months (out of a total of 12 months) of the rent for the year to 30 September 20X3 and 3 months (out of a total of 12 months) of the rent for the year to 30 September 20X4: (9/12 × £1,200) + (3/12 × £1,600) = £1,300.

7   **C**

VAT			
	£		£
Input VAT £64,200 × 20/120	10,700	Balance b/d	4,500
Bank	3,600	Output VAT £80,000 × 0.20	16,000
Balance c/d	6,200		
	———		———
	20,500		20,500

8   A

Payables ledger control account

	£		£
CB error (14,579 – 14,756)	180	Balance b/d	3,446
Receivables ledger control account	392		
Balance c/d	2,874		
	3,446		3,446

9   C

10   C

All three items are limitations of a trial balance.

Figures in the trial balance are not necessarily the final figures to be reported in the financial statements; they are subject to year-end adjustments.

Errors of commission (where an entry has been posted to the wrong account) are not identified by the trial balance since an equal debit and credit entry are still posted.

Although a trial balance can identify if double entry has broken down, it does not indicate in which accounts wrong entries were made.

35   DAYTIME

(a)   Complete the following statements:

On 01/04/X7, the commission receivable account shows a **debit** balance of **£3,200**. On 31/03/X8 the commission receivable account shows an adjustment for **accrued income** of **£2,800**.

(b)   Calculate the commission receivable for the year ended 31 March 20X8:

£22,400.

(c)   The bank summary for the year shows payments for telephone expenses of £1,896.

Update the telephone expense account for this, showing clearly the balance carried down.

Telephone expenses

Reversal of prepaid expenses	125		
Bank	1,896		
		Statement of profit or loss	2,021
	2,021		2,021

(d)   The amount to be transferred to the statement of profit or loss for telephone expenses will be **£110 greater** than the figure in (c).

Telephone expenses will show as a **debit** balance in the statement of profit or loss in the general ledger.

36   NIGHTIME

(a)   Complete the following statements:

On 01/01/X8, the rental income account shows a **credit** balance of **£1,800**. On 31/12/X8 the rental income account shows an adjustment for **prepaid income** of **£2,000**.

(b)   Calculate the rental income for the year ended 31 December 20X8:

£17,800.

(c)   The bank summary for the year shows payments for office expenses of £2,600.

Update the telephone expense account for this, showing clearly the amount transferred to the statement of profit or loss.

Office expenses

Bank	2,600	Reversal of accrued expenses	120
		Statement of profit or loss	2,480
	2,600		2,600

(d)   The amount to be transferred to the statement of profit or loss for office expenses will be **£800 greater** than the figure in (c).

Office expenses will show as a **debit** balance in the statement of profit or loss in the general ledger.

37   COLETTE

(a)   **General expenses**

Date	Description	Dr	Date	Description	Cr
			1/1/20X8	Accrued expenses reversal	£1,000

(b)   On the 31st December 20X8 the general ledger account for general expenses shows a credit entry for prepaid expenses carried down of £750 .

(c)   £6,750.

38 MAIKI

(a) **Sundry expenses**

Date	Description	Dr	Date	Description	Cr
1/4/20X6	Prepaid expenses reversal	£1,500			

(b) On the 31st March 20X7 the general ledger account for sundry expenses shows a debit entry for accrued expenses carried down of £500 .

(c) £13,500 .

39 RENTAL EXPENSES

(a) Calculate the value of the adjustment required for rental expenses as at 31 March 20X7.

£4,025 (Calculated as: (9/12 × £1,500) + £2,900)

(b) Update the rental expenses account.

Rental expenses

Prepaid expenses (reversal)	1,800	Prepaid expenses	4,025
Bank	10,550	Statement of profit or loss	8,325
	12,350		12,350

40 BANK RECONCILIATION I

Adjustment	Amount £	Debit/Credit
Adjustment for (1)	82	Cr
Adjustment for (2)	90	Dr
Adjustment for (4)	1,750	Dr

Key answer tips

Cash book

Balance b/d	5,472	Adjustment (1)	82
Adjustment (2)	90		
Adjustment (4)	1,750		
		Balance c/d	7,230
	7,312		7,312

Balance of bank account	5,250
Uncleared lodgements	1,980
	7,230

41 BANK RECONCILIATION II

Adjustment	Amount £	Debit/Credit
Adjustment for (2)	106	Cr
Adjustment for (3)	350	Dr
Adjustment for (4)	1,645	Dr

Key answer tips

Cash book

Balance b/d	103	Adjustment (2)	106
Adjustment (3)	350		
Adjustment (4)	1,645		
		Balance c/d	1,992
	2,098		2,098

Balance of bank account	363
Uncleared lodgements	1,629
	1,992

42   BANK RECONCILIATION III

C

43   PAYABLES LEDGER CONTROL ACCOUNT I

	Add/Subtract	£
Total from list of balances		52,750
Adjustment for (a)	Subtract	8,370
Adjustment for (b)	Subtract	540
Adjustment for (c)	Add	750
Adjustment for (d)	Add	462
Adjustment for (e)	Add	1,902
Adjustment for (f)	Add	540
Revised total to agree with PLCA		47,494

44   PAYABLES LEDGER CONTROL ACCOUNT II

	Add/Subtract	£
Total from list of balances		132,589
Adjustment for (a)	Add	445
Adjustment for (b)	Subtract	4,340
Adjustment for (c)	Subtract	1,200
Adjustment for (d)	Subtract	132
Adjustment for (e)	Add	2,100
Adjustment for (f)	Add	120
Revised total to agree with PLCA		129,582

45 RECEIVABLES LEDGER CONTROL ACCOUNT I

	Add/Subtract	£
Total from list of balances		31,820
Adjustment for (a)	Subtract	73
Adjustment for (b)	Add	280
Adjustment for (c)	Subtract	5,542
Adjustment for (d)	Add	3,090
Adjustment for (e)	Add	935
Adjustment for (f)	Add	450
Revised total to agree with RLCA		30,960

46 RECEIVABLES LEDGER CONTROL ACCOUNT II

	Add/Subtract	£
Total from list of balances		31,100
Adjustment for (a)	Add	65
Adjustment for (b)	Subtract	280
Adjustment for (c)	Subtract	1,170
Adjustment for (d)	Add	3,600
Adjustment for (e)	Subtract	99
Adjustment for (f)	Subtract	100
Revised total to agree with RLCA		33,116

47 BRODIE

(a) **Journal**

	Dr £	Cr £
Closing inventory – SPL	10,000	
Closing inventory – SoFP		10,000
Closing inventory – SoFP	9,800	
Closing inventory – SPL		9,800

(b) **Journal**

	Dr £	Cr £
Depreciation expense	8,052	
Provision for accumulated depreciation		8,052

(c)   The revised carrying amount as at 31 March 20X9 is £72,468

Key answer tip

Carrying amount as at 1 April 20X8	£80,520
Less: Depreciation charge for the year to 31 March 20X9	£8,052
Carrying amount as at 31 March 20X9	£72,468

(d)   **Journal**

	Dr £	Cr £
Payables	21,456	
Receivables		21,456

PRODUCE AND EXTEND THE TRIAL BALANCE

48   MULTIPLE CHOICE QUESTIONS

1   C

2   A

3   B

4   B

5   A

49   EXPENSES LEDGER ACCOUNTS I

Administration expenses

Bank	7,190	Reversal of accrued expenses	790
		Statement of profit or loss	4,600
		Prepaid expenses	1,800
	7,190		7,190

Selling expenses

Reversal of prepaid expenses	475	Statement of profit or loss	9,275
Bank	7,900		
Accrued expenses	900		
	9,275		9,275

Extract from trial balance as at 31 March 20X1.

Account	£	Dr £	Cr £
Accruals			900
Capital	6,000		6,000
Wages and salaries	850	850	
Selling expenses		9,275	
Drawings	11,000	11,000	
Administration expenses		4,600	
Interest received	70		70
Machinery at cost	5,600	5,600	
Machinery accumulated depreciation	4,200		4,200
Prepayments		1,800	

50 EXPENSES LEDGER ACCOUNTS II

Electricity expenses

Bank	10,539	Reversal of accrued expenses	2,815
		Statement of profit or loss	6,152
		Prepaid expenses	1,572
	10,539		10,539

Rental expenses

Reversal of prepaid expenses	6,250	Statement of profit or loss	75,000
Bank	62,500		
Accrued expenses	6,250		
	75,000		75,000

Extract from trial balance as at 31 March 20X6.

Account	£	Dr £	Cr £
Accruals			6,250
Accumulated depreciation – Office equipment	17,921		17,921
Depreciation charge	3,805	3,805	
Drawings	22,400	22,400	
Electricity		6,152	
Interest received	129		129
Office Equipment – cost	42,784	42,784	
Rental		75,000	
Stationery	2,800	2,800	
Prepayments		1,572	

51 EXPENSES LEDGER ACCOUNTS III

Telephone expenses

Bank	12,645	Reversal of accrued expenses	4,375
		Statement of profit or loss	6,844
		Prepaid expenses	1,426
	12,645		12,645

Rates expenses

Reversal of prepaid expenses	5,000	Statement of profit or loss	96,000
Bank	82,750		
Accrued expenses	8,250		
	96,000		96,000

Extract from trial balance as at 31 December 20X8

Account	£	Dr £	Cr £
Accruals			8,250
Accumulated depreciation – Machinery	15,437		15,437
Bank charges	2,897	2,897	
Capital	27,000		27,000
Discounts allowed	520	520	
Light and heat	4,000	4,000	
Machinery – cost	41,697	41,697	
Prepayments		1,426	
Rates		96,000	
Telephone		6,844	

52   RENT

(a)   Statement of profit or loss: £2,250

Prepayment: £600

Key answer tips

The financial year is 1 October 20X6 to 30 September 20X7. Out of the rental charge for 1 January – 31 December 20X6 three out of the total of twelve months relates to the financial year. Out of the rental charge for 1 January – 31 December 20X7 nine out of the total of twelve months relates to the financial year. The remaining three months of that rental charge have been prepaid as at the financial year end date 30 September 20X7.

Statement of profit or loss rental charge:

3/12 × £1,800	= £450
9/12 × £2,400	= £1,800
Total rental charge	= £2,250
Prepayment:	
3/12 × £2,400	= £600

(b)

Accrued at 30 September 20X7	Charge to the statement of profit or loss year ended 30 September 20X7
£175	£2,650

Key answer tips

The financial year is 1 October 20X6 to 30 September 20X7. As at 1 October 20X6 there is an opening accrual for £200 – this relates to expense that occurred in the prior year but which will be paid in the current year. In accordance with the accruals concept the expense would have been recognised in the prior year when it was incurred and so it should not be recognised again when it is paid in the current year.

No electricity expense has been recognised for the month of September 20X7 therefore it needs to be accrued for. The accrual will be estimated based on the most recent bill which was for £525 for 3 months charge.

Statement of profit or loss electricity charge:

£2,650

£600 – £200 (opening accrual) + £800 + £750 + £525 + £175 (estimated closing accrual)

Accrual:

£175 (1/3 × £525)

(c) **Extract** from trial balance as at 30 September 20X7.

Account	£	Dr £	Cr £
Accruals			175
Capital	100,000		100,000
Wages and salaries	25,000	25,000	
Rental expense		2,250	
Drawings	5,000	5,000	
Electricity expense		2,650	
Interest paid	950	950	
Computer equipment at cost	4,575	4,575	
Computer equipment accumulated depreciation	1,550		1,550
Prepayments		600	

53 ANDREAS

Extract from trial balance as at 30 December 20X6.

Account	£	Dr £	Cr £
Bank		11,000	
Capital	24,198		24,198
Discounts received			300
Electricity		350	
Fixtures & fittings at cost	11,000	11,000	
Fixtures & fittings accumulated depreciation	2,400		2,400
Irrecoverable debt expense		1,987	
Misc. expense	2,600	2,600	
Prepaid expense		100	
Prepaid income			500
Rental income			3,000
Stationery	55	55	

(b)

Adjustment number	Amount (£)	Add	Deduct
1	157		✓
2	100		✓

(c)

Adjustment number	Amount (£)	Debit	Credit
2	100		✓
3	350		✓
4	200	✓	

54   KYLE

(a)   **Extract** from trial balance as at 31 December 20X6.

Account	£	Dr £	Cr £
Accruals			250
Capital	25,000		25,000
Wages and salaries	2,400	2,400	
Allowance for doubtful receivables adjustment			160
Receivables	11,000	11,000	
Drawings		1,000	
Entertainment expense	70	70	
Computer equipment at cost	2,600	2,600	
Computer equipment accumulated depreciation	1,200		1,200
Commission received			650
General expenses		2,500	
Discount allowed		575	

(b)

Adjustment number	Amount (£)	Add	Deduct
1	450		✓
3	100		✓

(c)

Adjustment number	Amount (£)	Debit	Credit
2	100	✓	
4	200		✓

55 JACKSONS

(a) **Extract** from extended trial balance

	Ledger balances		Adjustments	
	Dr £	Cr £	Dr £	Cr £
Allowance for doubtful receivables		365		
Bank	4,300			1,600
Closing inventory – SoFP			17,700	
Closing inventory – SPL				17,700
Depreciation charge				
Irrecoverable debts			220	
Loan		4,000		
Loan interest	240			
Plant and machinery – accumulated depreciation		22,000		
Sales		210,000		
Receivables ledger control account	24,500		400	220
Suspense		1,200	1,600	400
VAT		5,600		

(b)

Account	Debit/Credit
Statement of profit or loss	Debit
Loan interest	Credit
Transfer of loan interest charge for year to SPL	

56 PERCY

(a) **Journal**

	Dr £	Cr £
Irrecoverable debt/Allowance for doubtful receivables adjustment	500	
Allowance for doubtful receivables		500
Irrecoverable debt	715	
Receivables ledger control account		715

(b)   **Journal**

	Dr £	Cr £
Motor repairs	880	
Suspense		880

(c)   **Journal**

	Dr £	Cr £
Closing inventory – statement of financial position	31,610	
Closing inventory – statement of profit or loss		31,610

Tutorial note

Inventory is valued at the lower of cost and net realisable value. The original inventory value of £33,821 needs to be adjusted as some inventory has been identified in which its cost exceeds its net realisable value. Therefore the cost of £5,211 needs to be removed and revalued at the lower NRV of £3,000.

33,821 – 5,211 + 3,000 = 31,610.

(d)   **Journal**

	Dr £	Cr £
VAT	4,375	
Suspense		4,375
VAT	4,375	
Suspense		4,375

Key answer tip

Suspense account

Balance b/d	9,630	**Motor repairs**	880
		VAT	4,375
		VAT	4,375
	9,630		9,630

57   MERCURY DELIVERIES

Journal

	Dr £	Cr £
Stationery	275	
Suspense		275

Journal

	Dr £	Cr £
Closing inventory – SFP	34,962	
Closing inventory – SPL		34,962

Journal

	Dr £	Cr £
Irrecoverable debt	210	
Receivables ledger control account		210

Journal

	Dr £	Cr £
Suspense	6,400	
VAT		6,400
Suspense	6,400	
VAT		6,400

Key answer tip

Suspense account

VAT	6,400	Balance b/d	12,525
VAT	6,400	Stationery	275
	12,800		12,800

58   EVANS AND CO

(a)

	£	Debit	Credit
Capital	50,000		50,000
Purchases	83,468	83,468	
Revenue	159,407		159,407
Purchase returns	2,693		2,693
Sales returns	3,090	3,090	
RLCA	25,642	25,642	
PLCA	31,007		31,007
Drawings	25,500	25,500	
Machinery – Cost	45,900	45,900	
Machinery – Accumulated depreciation	15,925		15,925
Rent and rates	15,600	15,600	
Light and heat	2,466	2,466	
Motor expenses	2,603	2,603	
Loan	12,500		12,500
Interest	1,250	1,250	
Discounts received	400		400
Irrecoverable debts	1,300	1,300	
Allowances for doubtful receivables	2,572		2,572
Salaries	77,921	77,921	
Bank overdraft	3,876		3,876
Suspense			**6,360**
Totals		284,740	284,740

(b)

		Dr £	Cr
(i)	Drawings	1,000	
	Salaries		1,000
(ii)	Suspense	280	
	Purchases		280
(iii)	Suspense	70	
	VAT		70
(iv)	Suspense	3,175	
	Bank		3,175
	Suspense	3,175	
	Bank		3,175
(v)	Electricity	340	
	Suspense		340

59   RACHEL EDMUNDSON

(a)

	£	Debit	Credit
Accruals	4,820		4,820
Prepayments	2,945	2,945	
Motor expenses	572	572	
Administration expenses	481	481	
Light and heat	1,073	1,073	
Revenue	48,729		48,729
Purchases	26,209	26,209	
RLCA	5,407	5,407	
PLCA	3,090		3,090
Rent	45	45	
Purchase returns	306		306
Discounts allowed	567	567	
Capital	10,000		10,000
Loan	15,000		15,000
Interest paid	750	750	
Drawings	4,770	4,770	
Motor vehicles – cost	19,000	19,000	
Motor vehicle – accumulated depreciation	2,043		2,043
VAT control	2,995		2,995
Wages	20,000	20,000	
Suspense account		**5,164**	
Totals		86,983	86,983

(b)

		Dr £	Cr £
(i)	Suspense	5,000	
	Capital		5,000
(ii)	Suspense	385	
	Receivables ledger control account		385
(iii)	VAT	193	
	Suspense		193
(iv)	Rent	4,500	
	Suspense		4,500
	Rent	4,500	
	Suspense		4,500
(v)	Electricity	1,356	
	Suspense		1,356

60 BUSTER

(a) **Journal**

	Dr £	Cr £
Motor expenses	4,500	
Motor vehicles at cost		4,500

(b) **Journal**

	Dr £	Cr £
Office sundries	16	
Suspense		16

(c) **Journal**

	Dr £	Cr £
Closing inventory – statement of financial position	189,320	
Closing inventory – statement of profit or loss		189,320

Tutorial note

Inventory is valued at the lower of cost and net realisable value. The selling price is given as £227,184. To get to the selling price, 20% of the value of the cost is added to the cost. The cost of £189,320 has been calculated by dividing the selling price by 120 and then multiplying by 100.

(227,184/120) × 100 = 189,320

The value of closing inventory, in accordance with IAS 2 is £189,320.

(d)   **Journal**

	Dr £	Cr £
Receivables	1,720	
Discounts allowed		1,720
Discounts allowed	1,270	
Receivables		1,270

61   PAYROLL COSTS

Step 1 – Account for the total wages expense to the employer.

Debit	Wages expense
Credit	Wages and salaries control

Step 2 – Account for the payment of net pay to the employees.

Debit	Wages and salaries control
Credit	Bank

Step 3 – Account for the PAYE, employer's NIC and employees' NIC payable to HM Revenue and Customs.

Debit	Wages and salaries control
Credit	HMRC payable

Step 4 – Account for the employees' pension contributions due to the pension fund.

Debit	Wages and salaries control
Credit	Pension payable

62   CARTERS

Extended trial balance

Ledger account	Ledger balances		Adjustments		Statement of profit or loss		Statement of financial position	
	Dr £	Cr £	Dr £	Cr £	Dr £	Cr £	Dr £	Cr £
Allowance for doubtful receivables		1,300	600					700
Allowance for doubtful receivables adjustment				600		600		
Bank	28,380			500			27,880	
Capital		4,530						4,530
Closing inventory			40,000	40,000		40,000	40,000	
Depreciation charge			20,500		20,500			
Office expenses	69,550			500	69,050			
Opening inventory	26,000				26,000			
Payroll expenses	31,150			150	31,000			
Purchases	188,000		900		188,900			
Payables ledger control account		29,900						29,900
Revenue		436,000				436,000		
Receivables ledger control account	36,000						36,000	
Selling expenses	67,000				67,000			
Suspense		250	1,150	900				
VAT		9,800						9,800
Vehicles at cost	62,000						62,000	
Vehicles accumulated depreciation		26,300		20,500				46,800
Net profit					74,150			74,150
	508,080	508,080	63,150	63,150	476,600	476,600	165,880	165,880

63   GREENWOODS

Extended trial balance

Ledger account	Ledger balances		Adjustments		Statement of profit or loss		Statement of financial position	
	Dr £	Cr £	Dr £	Cr £	Dr £	Cr £	Dr £	Cr £
Accruals		2,300		425				2,725
Advertising	1,800				1,800			
Bank	7,912		1,175				9,087	
Capital		40,000						40,000
Closing inventory			6,590	6,590		6,590	6,590	
Depreciation charge			821		821			
Drawings	14,700						14,700	
Fixtures and fittings – accumulated depreciation		945		821				1,766
Fixtures and fittings – cost	6,099						6,099	
Interest	345				345			
Light and heat	1,587		706		2,293			
Loan		10,000						10,000
Opening inventory	5,215				5,215			
Prepayments	485		927	281			1,131	
Purchases	75,921				75,921			
PLCA		14,000						14,000
Rent and rates	38,000			927	37,073			
Revenue		145,825				145,825		
RLCA	9,500			1,175			8,325	
VAT control account		11,453						11,453
Wages	62,959				62,959			
Loss						34,012	34,012	
	224,523	224,523	10,219	10,219	186,427	186,427	79,944	79,944

64 WIDGETS

Extended trial balance

Ledger account	Ledger balances		Adjustments	
	Dr £	Cr £	Dr £	Cr £
Accruals		1,330		300
Advertising	1,800			
Bank	7,912			
Capital		50,000		
Closing inventory			11,890	11,890
Depreciation charge				
Drawings	14,700			
Fixtures and fittings – accumulated depreciation		945		
Fixtures and fittings – cost	6,099			
Irrecoverable debts	345			
Allowance for doubtful receivables adjustment				295
Electricity	1,587		300	
Loan	10,000			
Opening inventory	5,215			
Prepayment			12,500	
Allowance for doubtful receivables		485	295	
Purchases	78,921			
Purchase returns				2,000
PLCA		14,000	2,400	
Rent	25,000			12,500
Revenue		145,825		
RLCA	9,500			
VAT control account		11,453		400
Wages	62,959			
	224,038	224,038	27,385	27,385

Key answer tips

(a)   RLCA 9,500 × 2% = 190. Allowance currently 485, therefore debit with £295 to make it equal £190

(c)   The prepayment for the year end is 10/12 × 15,000 = 12,500. For November and December X5 = 2/12 × 15,000 = 2,500. Total rental charge for the year = (10/12 × 12,000) + 2,500 = £12,500

(e)   Accrual for November and December. 2/3 × 450 = £300

65   BINS 4 U

Extended trial balance

Ledger account	Ledger balances		Adjustments	
	Dr £	**Cr** £	**Dr** £	**Cr** £
Accruals		2,900		60
Admin expenses	900			
Allowance for doubtful receivables		1,040	539	
Bank overdraft		2,763		
Cash	246			
Capital		40,000		
Closing inventory			17,795	17,795
Drawings	13,475			
Water	2,197			60
Light and heat	2,018			
Loan		12,000		
Opening inventory	4,600			
Plant and machinery – accumulated depreciation		7,075		
Plant and machinery – cost	20,370			
Prepayments	1,200		6,250	
Purchases	100,159			
Rent	12,500			6,250
Rates	8,500			
Salaries	46,376			
Revenue		151,606		
Sales returns			600	
RLCA	10,745			720
Irrecoverable debts	850			
Allowance for doubtful receivables adjustment				539
VAT control account		6,752	120	
	224,136	224,136	25,364	25,364

Key answer tips

(b)   RLCA 10,745 − 720 = 10,025 × 5% = 501. Provision currently 1,040, therefore 539 needed to reduce provision

(c)   The prepayment for rent is 7,500 × 10/12 = 6,250

(e)   Accrue 1/3 × £180

66   TEAPOT

(a)   (i)

	Debit ✓	Credit ✓	Statement of financial position	Statement of profit or loss
Prepayments	✓		✓	
Discounts allowed	✓			✓

(ii)   Rental expenses incorrectly included within electricity expenses **will not** be identified by the initial trial balance.

The wrong economic lifetime used within the depreciation charges **will not** be identified by the initial trial balance.

A receipt from a credit customer which was correctly entered into the bank, but no other entries were made **will** be identified by the initial trial balance.

Drawings during the year that was debited to cash and to the drawings account **will** be identified by the initial trial balance.

(b)

Bank reconciliation as at 31 March 20X8	
	£
Balance as per the bank statement	61.52 Cr
Add	
JJ Nelli	500.00
Less	
Tony's Sweets	(170.00)
Balance as per the cash book	391.52 Dr

(c)

Account Name	Debit £	Credit £
Closing inventory: statement of financial position	5,740	
Closing inventory: statement of profit or loss		5,740
Bank	10,000	
Capital		10,000
Electricity	100	
Suspense		100
Receivables ledger control account	200	
Suspense		200

(d)

Account name	Ledger balances		Adjustments		Statement of profit or loss		Statement of financial position	
	Dr	Cr	Dr	Cr	Dr	Cr	Dr	Cr
Payables ledger control		6,190						6,190
Receivables ledger control	525						525	
Value Added Tax		745						745
Bank	2,435						2,435	
Capital		15,000						15,000
Sales revenue		82,137				82,137		
Purchases	37,745			75	37,670			
Opening inventory	11,325				**11,325**			
Shop wages	21,212		210		21,422			
Accrued expenses				210				210
Heat and light	1,710				1,710			
Rent	6,340				6,340			
Prepayment of rent	375						375	
Closing inventory			12,710	12,710		**12,710**	**12,710**	
Shop fittings at cost	11,000		75				11,075	
Shop fittings: depreciation charges	2,625				2,625			
Shop fittings: accumulated depreciation		5,250						5,250
Loss on disposal of non-current asset	100				**100**			
Irrecoverable debts	60				60			
Drawings	13,870						13,870	
Profit for the year					13,595			**13,595**
Total	109,322	109,322	12,995	12,995	94,847	94,847	40,990	40,990

67 RZ TRAINING

(a) (i)

Statement	True ✓	False ✓
Opening inventory will be included in both the statement of profit or loss and statement of financial position columns.		✓
Drawings will be in the credit column of the statement of financial position.		✓
Losses for the year will be shown in the credit column within the statement of profit or loss.	✓	
The total of debits and credits in the adjustment columns will be equal.	✓	

(ii)

Statement	Assets	Liabilities	Capital
RZ Training buys computer equipment for cash	No effect (increase and decrease to assets)	No effect	No effect
Jakki withdrew cash from RZ Training to buy her daughter a new puppy	Decrease	No effect	Decrease (drawings increases)

(b)

Errors	Payables Ledger control account		Individual payables accounts		No effect ✓
	Debit £	Credit £	Debit £	Credit £	
A credit note from Jasmine Gubta for £422.10 (including VAT) has been posted to Josh Grealish's account in the payables ledger.					✓
A credit note for discount received of £36 (including VAT) has been entered into Declan Curry's individual account but has been omitted from the payables' ledger control account completely.	£36				
In the payables' ledger, a purchase invoice for £180 including VAT was posted to the wrong side of G Southfence's account.				£360	
The total column in the purchases daybook has been overcast by £300.	£300				

(c)

Trial Balance for M Wie as at 31 March 20X8				
	Ledger balances		Adjustments	
	Dr	Cr	Dr	Cr
	£	£	£	£
Accumulated depreciation		447,938		
Administration expenses	739,800			
Cash at bank	33,946			19,200
Capital		1,494,522		
Depreciation charge	54,900			
Wages	821,074			
Drawings	77,818			
Irrecoverable debts	2,738			
Non-current assets at cost	2,178,348			
Opening inventory	17,338			
Other expenses	708,958			
Purchases	420,886			
Rent	170,894		19,200	
Sales revenue		3,251,284		
VAT		60,512		
Trade payables		94,474	3,000	
Trade receivables	121,030			2,000
Closing inventory SFP			16,856	
Closing inventory SPL				16,856
Suspense	1,000		2,000	3,000
	5,348,730	5,348,730	41,056	41,056

(d)

Extract of the trial balance as at 31 March 20X9		
	Dr	Cr
	£	£
Deferred income		500
Allowance for doubtful receivables		900
VAT		270
Discount received		910
Loss on disposal of NCA	125	
Increase in allowance for doubtful receivables	50	

68   CAFETIERE

(a)   (i)

	Debit ✓	Credit ✓	Statement of financial position ✓	Statement of profit or loss ✓
Bank overdraft		✓	✓	
Capital introduced		✓	✓	

(ii)

Statement	True ✓	False ✓
In the statement of profit or loss columns in the extended trial balance, If the debits column is larger than the credits column, the business has made a profit for the year.		✓
In a bank reconciliation, outstanding lodgements will cause the bank statement to be higher than the cash book balance.		✓
VAT on purchase returns is credited to the VAT control account.	✓	
In a partnership, the appropriation of profit will be credited to the partners' capital accounts.		✓

(b)

Errors	Receivables ledger control account Debit £	Receivables ledger control account Credit £	Individual receivables accounts Debit £	Individual receivables accounts Credit £	No effect ✓
An invoice of £72 has been entered twice in D Asher-Smith's individual account.				72	
In the receivables ledger, an invoice for £360 was posted to the wrong side of S Cram's account.			720		
A credit note to M. Farah for £130 has been posted to J Ennis' account in the receivables ledger.					✓
The total column in the sales daybook has been undercast by £300.	300				

(c)

Account name	Debit £	Credit £
Closing inventory: statement of financial position	11,480	
Closing inventory: statement of profit or loss		11,480
Bank	20,000	
Receivables ledger control account		20,000
Broadband expense	500	
Suspense		500
Payables ledger control account	200	
Suspense		200

(d)

Trial balance extract as at 31 March 20X9		
	Dr £	Cr £
Prepayments	250	
Allowance for doubtful receivables		1,000
VAT	600	
Discount received		200
Gain on disposal of NCA		160
Movement in allowance for doubtful receivables		500

PRODUCE FINANCIAL STATEMENTS FOR SOLE TRADERS AND PARTNERSHIPS

69 PG TRADING

(a)

PG Trading			
Statement of financial position as at 30 September 20X7			
	£	£	£
Non-current assets	**Cost**	**Depreciation**	**Carrying amount**
Machinery	15,900	5,800	10,100
Current assets			
Inventory		11,000	
Trade receivables (£17,900 – £800)		17,100	
Bank		5,000	
Prepayments		5,100	
		38,200	
Current liabilities			
Trade payables	15,900		
Accruals	6,000		
VAT	1,500		
		23,400	
Net current assets			14,800
Net assets			24,900
Financed by:			
Opening capital			20,000
Add: Net profit			7,900
Less: Drawings			3,000
Closing capital			24,900

(b) £24,900

70 INVENTORY TRADING

(a)

Inventory Trading			
Statement of financial position as at 31 March 20X1			
	£	£	£
Non-current assets	**Cost**	**Depreciation**	**Carrying amount**
Motor vehicles	39,000	18,500	20,500
Current assets			
Inventory		20,000	
Trade receivables (£78,920 – £1,200)		77,720	
Bank		4,100	
Cash		670	
		102,490	
Current liabilities			
Trade payables	28,500		
VAT	4,000		
Accruals	2,500		
		35,000	
Net current assets			67,490
Net assets			87,990
Financed by:			
Opening capital			74,390
Add: Net profit			15,000
Less: Drawings			1,400
Closing capital			87,990

(b) As a current asset.

71   WINSTON TRADING

Winston Trading			
Statement of financial position as at 30 June 20X8			
	£	£	£
Non-current assets	**Cost**	**Depreciation**	**Carrying amount**
Equipment	17,500	4,500	13,000
Current assets			
Inventory		7,850	
Trade receivables (£7,800 – £840)		6,960	
Prepayments		3,200	
		18,010	
Current liabilities			
Payables (£6,800 + £1,450)	8,250		
VAT	2,950		
Accruals	750		
Bank	1,250		
		13,200	
Net current assets			4,810
Net assets			17,810
Financed by:			
Opening capital			17,000
Add: Net profit			8,810
Less: Drawings			8,000
Closing capital			17,810

72   BALFOUR

Balfour

Statement of financial position as at 30 June 20X6

	£	£	£
Non-current assets	**Cost**	**Depreciation**	**Carrying amount**
Motor vehicles	45,000	20,000	25,000
Current assets			
Inventory		17,500	
Trade receivables (£68,550 – £1,450)		67,100	
Cash		500	
		85,100	
Current liabilities			
Bank	2,250		
Trade payables	23,750		
Accruals	3,150		
VAT	3,500		
		32,650	
Net current assets			52,450
Net assets			77,450
Financed by:			
Opening capital			85,000
Less: Net loss			4,350
Less: Drawings			3,200
Closing capital			77,450

73 ROG

(a) (i) £155,000 (£160,150 – £5,150)

(ii) £72,750 (£71,170 + £1,580)

(b) **Statement of profit or loss for ROG for the year ended 31 March 20X7**

	£	£
Revenue		155,000
Cost of sales		
Opening inventory	2,980	
Purchases	72,750	
Closing inventory	(3,480)	
		72,250
Gross profit		82,750
Sundry income		
Disposal		320
Expenses		
Rent	7,200	
Payroll expenses	14,000	
Allowance for doubtful receivables adjustment	220	
Advertising	2,000	
Miscellaneous expenses	1,500	
Depreciation charges	6,600	
Total expenses		31,520
Profit/(loss) for the year		51,550

(c)

Capital

	£		£
Loss	15,500	**Balance b/d**	**42,000**
Drawings	2,800		
Balance c/d	23,700		
Total	**42,000**	**Total**	**42,000**

74 OLIVIA

(a)   (i)   £689,220 (£704,440 – £15,220)

      (ii)   £387,861 (£400,746 – £12,885)

(b)   **Statement of profit or loss for Olivia for the year ended 31 March 20X7**

	£	£
Revenue		689,220
Cost of sales		
Opening inventory	41,211	
Purchases	387,861	
Closing inventory	(64,500)	
		364,572
Gross profit		324,648
Sundry income		
Allowance for doubtful receivables adjustment		750
Expenses		
Payroll expenses	113,326	
General expenses	72,900	
Motor expenses	14,633	
Disposal	3,870	
Depreciation charges	12,995	
Total expenses		217,724
Profit/(loss) for the year		107,674

(c)

	Increase ✓	Decrease ✓	No change ✓
Assets		✓	
Liabilities			✓
Capital		✓	

75   RACHAEL, ED AND MATTY

Partnership appropriation account for the year ended 30 June 20X9

	£
Profit for the year	220,000
Salaries:	
Rachael	18,000
Ed	0
Matty	36,000
Interest on capital:	
Rachael	2,000
Ed	2,000
Matty	2,000
Sales commission:	
Rachael	8,250
Ed	6,800
Matty	4,715
Profit available for distribution	140,235

Profit share:	
Rachael (40% × £140,235)	56,094
Ed (40% × £140,235)	56,094
Matty (20% × £140,235)	28,047
Total residual profit distributed	140,235

76 NYAH, SHAUNA AND MOLLIE

Partnership appropriation account for the year ended 31 March 20Y0

	£
Profit for the year	70,000
Salaries:	
Nyah	25,000
Shauna	19,000
Mollie	0
Sales commission	
Nyah	1,100
Shauna	1,100
Mollie	1,100
Profit available for distribution	22,700

Profit share:	
Nyah (35% × £22,700)	7,945
Shauna (20% × £22,700)	4,540
Mollie (45% × £22,700)	10,215
Total residual profit distributed	22,700

77   EDWARD, JAKE AND BELLA

Partnership appropriation account for the year ended 31 December 20X0

	£
Profit for the year	52,000
Salaries:	
Edward	30,000
Jake	0
Bella	21,000
Sales commission:	
Edward	3,000
Jake	3,000
Bella	3,200
Interest on drawings:	
Edward	1,880
Jake	2,870
Bella	0
Residual profit / loss	-3,450

Profit / loss share:	
Edward (50% × −£3,450)	−1,725
Jake (20% × −£3,450)	−690
Bella (30% × −£3,450)	−1,035
Total residual profit / loss distributed	−3,450

78   GARY, MARK AND ROBBIE

Current accounts

	Gary £	Mark £	Robbie £		Gary £	Mark £	Robbie £
Drawings	34,000	30,000	58,000	Balance b/d	2,000	1,500	250
				Salaries	18,000	0	36,000
Balance c/d	23,000	6,500		Interest	5,000	3,000	3,750
				Profit share	32,000	32,000	16,000
				Balance c/d			2,000
	57,000	36,500	58,000		57,000	36,500	58,000

79 JOHN, JACKIE AND TEGAN

Current accounts

	John £	Jackie £	Tegan £		John £	Jackie £	Tegan £
Balance b/d	750			Balance b/d		1,900	600
Drawings	18,000	35,000	12,750	Salaries	11,000	16,500	0
Balance c/d	20,400	19,390	5,090	Interest	1,900	2,240	2,240
				Profit share	26,250	33,750	15,000
	39,150	54,390	17,840		39,150	54,390	17,840

80 LOUIS, CHERYL AND SIMON

Current accounts

	Louis £	Cheryl £	Simon £		Louis £	Cheryl £	Simon £
Drawings	25,000	10,200	31,000	Balance b/d	3,500	1,800	1,000
Balance c/d	39,500	4,600	9,400	Salaries	30,000	0	21,000
				Interest	1,000	1,000	400
				Profit share	30,000	12,000	18,000
	64,500	14,800	40,400		64,500	14,800	40,400

81 DEREK, JIN AND AHMED

Partnership Appropriation account for the year ended 31 March 20X8:

	£
Profit for the year	254,000
Salaries:	
Derek	20,000
Jin	24,000
Ahmed	0
Interest on capital:	
Derek	8,000
Jin	7,200
Ahmed	10,560
Interest on drawings:	
Derek	4,600
Jin	3,800
Ahmed	4,800
Profit available for distribution	197,440

Profit share:	
Derek (3 / 10 × £197,440)	59,232
Jin (3 / 10 × £197,440)	59,232
Ahmed (4 / 10 × £197,440)	78,976
Total residual profit distributed	197,440

82   JACOB AND OLIVER

Partnership Appropriation account for the year ended 31 December 20X8:

	£
Profit for the year	182,225
Salaries:	
Jacob	20,000
Oliver	20,000
Interest on capital:	
Jacob	2,800
Oliver	6,250
Sales commission:	
Jacob	1,560
Oliver	2,690
Interest on drawings:	
Jacob	2,275
Oliver	0
Profit available for distribution	131,200

Profit share:	
Jacob (£131,200 / 2)	65,600
Oliver (£131,200 / 2)	65,600
Total residual profit distributed	131,200

83   R & R TRADING

(a)

R & R Trading		
Statement of profit or loss for the year ended 30 September 20X7		
	£	£
Revenue (£173,050 – £2,200)		170,850
Opening inventory	17,700	
Purchases	98,000	
Closing inventory	–19,500	
Cost of goods sold		96,200
Gross profit		74,650
Less:		
Depreciation charge	7,100	
Discounts allowed	1,350	
General expenses	26,100	
Rent	7,300	
Wages	8,500	
Total expenses		50,350
Profit for the year		24,300

(b)

	£
Rita's share of the profit or loss (£24,300 × 55%)	13,365
Rita's final current account balance (£920 + £13,365 – £6,000)	8,285

84   OSMOND PARTNERSHIP

(a)

Osmond Partnership		
Statement of profit or loss for the year ended 31 March 20X1		
	£	£
Revenue (£164,000 – £1,500)		162,500
Opening inventory	3,450	
Purchases	125,000	
Closing inventory	–7,850	
Cost of goods sold		120,600
Gross profit		41,900
Add:		
Discounts received	900	
Disposal	450	
Total sundry income		1,350
Less:		
Depreciation charge	1,600	
Discounts allowed	345	
General expenses	2,950	
Rent	5,250	
Irrecoverable bad debt expense	295	
Wages	24,000	
Total expenses		34,440
Profit for the year		8,810

(b)

	£
Heather's share of the profit or loss (£8,810 × 50%)	4,405
Heather's final current account balance (–£400 + £4,405 – £3,250)	755

85 PERSEPHONE'S

(a)

Persephone's		
Statement of profit or loss for the year ended 30 June 20X8		
	£	£
Revenue		85,000
Opening inventory	9,100	
Purchases	38,700	
Closing inventory	−9,800	
Cost of goods sold		38,000
Gross profit		47,000
Plus:		
Allowance for doubtful receivables adjustment		1,000
Less:		
Depreciation charge	800	
General expenses	8,200	
Rent	5,900	
Wages	8,500	
Total expenses		23,400
Profit for the year		24,600

(b)

	Tina (£)	Cher (£)	Total (£)
Current account Tina (W) £2,257 + (£24,600 × 60%) − £2,054 Cher (W) £3,750 + (£24,600 × 40%) − £2,553	14,963	11,037	26,000
Capital account (Trial balance figures)	2,050	2,050	4,100
	17,013	13,087	30,100

86 SUAREZ PARTNERSHIP

(a)

Suarez Partnership		
Statement of profit or loss for the year ended 30 June 20X6		
	£	£
Revenue		108,000
Opening inventory	13,100	
Purchases (£70,600 – £2,350)	68,250	
Closing inventory	–12,500	
Cost of goods sold		68,850
Gross profit		39,150
Plus:		
Profit on disposal		225
Less:		
Depreciation charge	925	
General expenses	9,300	
Rent	6,000	
Wages	12,000	
Total expenses		28,225
Profit for the year		11,150

(b)

	Louis (£)	Emilio (£)	Total (£)
Current account Louis (W) £1,500 + (£11,150 × 50%) – £2,500 Emilio (W) – £200 + (£11,150 × 50%) – £2,500	4,575	2,875	7,450
Capital account	4,160	3,000	7,160
	8,735	5,875	14,610

87   JCR PARTNERSHIP

(i)

	Balance	Debit	Credit
June	£14,082		✓
Charlie	£7,108		✓

Workings:

June   900 + 19,182 – 6,000 = 14,082

Charlie –680 + 12,788 – 5,000 = 7,108

(ii)   **£23,400** (£26,400 – £3,000)

(iii)

JCR			
Statement of financial position as at 31 March 20X7.			
	£	£	£
Non-current assets	Cost	Accumulated depreciation	Carrying amount
Machinery	35,176	15,220	19,956
Current assets			
Closing inventory		22,000	
Receivables		23,400	
Prepaid expenses		5,414	
Bank		4,000	
		54,814	
Current liabilities			
Accrued expenses	4,080		
Payables	32,000		
VAT	5,500		
		41,580	
Net current assets			13,234
Net assets			**33,190**
Financed by:			
	June	Charlie	Total
Capital accounts	7,000	5,000	12,000
Current accounts	14,082	7,108	21,190
	21,082	12,108	**33,190**

88 FORCE PARTNERSHIP

(i)

	Balance	Debit	Credit
Tracey	£6,047	✓	
Matilda	£5,548	✓	

Workings:

Tracey   1,000 – 3,797 – 3,250 = –6,047

Matilda   –400 – 1,898 – 3,250 = –5,548

(ii)   **£26,960** (£27,800 - £840)

(iii)

FORCE			
Statement of financial position as at 31 March 20X7.			
	£	£	£
Non-current assets	Cost	Accumulated depreciation	Carrying amount
Equipment	18,100	4,500	13,600
Current assets			
Closing inventory		6,500	
Receivables		26,960	
Prepaid expenses		3,200	
		36,660	
Current liabilities			
Payables	6,800		
Accrued expenses	750		
VAT	17,555		
Bank	1,250		
		26,355	
Net current assets			10,305
Net assets			**23,905**
Financed by:			
	Tracey	**Matilda**	**Total**
Capital accounts	18,000	17,500	35,500
Current accounts	6,047	5,548	11,595
	11,953	11,952	**23,905**

Note: The balances on both Tracey's and Matilda's current accounts are negative (debit balances), shown when arriving at the totals of the capital and current accounts.

INTERPRET FINANCIAL STATEMENTS USING PROFITABILITY RATIOS

89 WHEELSTOGO

(a)

	True ✓	False ✓
Ratio analysis is the only way to make conclusions about the financial performance or position of an entity		✓
Ratios are only useful if comparative information (i.e. prior year ratios, industry averages) is available	✓	
Ratios give the users the ability to accurately determine the future performance of a business		✓

(b) (i)

Return on capital employed	46.41% 65,350 / (106,200+34,600)
Gross profit margin	29.22% 96,180 / 329,160

(ii) The selling expenses / revenue percentage shows **an improvement** when compared to the previous year's figures.

(c) **Scenario 1**

Your company has managed to negotiate a lower price with a main supplier of your inventory. This has not affected the quality of goods you receive.

	Increase ✓	Unchanged ✓	Decrease ✓
Return on capital employed	✓		
Gross profit percentage	✓		

Scenario 2

The wage rates of administration staff have risen in line with others in the industry. The amount / skills level of the labour has been unaffected.

	Increase ✓	Unchanged ✓	Decrease ✓
Net profit percentage			✓
Cost of sales percentage		✓	

90   PENTOP

(a)

Statement	True ✓	False ✓
The interpretation of an entity's financial statements using ratios is only useful for existing shareholders.		✓
Return on capital employed is calculated as: gross profit/capital employed × 100		✓
A disadvantage of ratios is that they are based on previous performance which may not be valid for making predictions about the future.	✓	
All other things being equal, if gross profit percentage increases, then the net profit percentage will decrease.		✓

(b)   (i)

Return on capital employed (%)	24.91% (57,260 / (87,500+142,400))
Net profit margin (%)	10.93% (57,260 / 523,8000)

(c)   (ii)

Statement	True ✓	False ✓
The rise could have been caused by the business taking on a new employee within the accounts department.	✓	
The rise could have been caused by revenue rising during the year due to increased advertising expenditure in the previous year.		✓

91 RUNPARK

(a)

Statement	True ✓	False ✓
The interpretation of an entity's financial statements using ratios is only useful for lenders.		✓
Achieving a gross profit margin of more than 5% is always considered an improvement in performance.		✓
A disadvantage of ratios is that they can be distorted through issues such as seasonality or creative accounting.	✓	
Gross profit margin, net profit margin and return on capital employed must be disclosed on the face of the financial statements each year.		✓

(b) (i)

Return on capital employed (%)	31.68% (77,260 / (47,500 + 196,400))
Cost of sales / revenue ratio (%)	53.84% ((223,400 – 103,120 / 223,400)

(ii)

Statement	True ✓	False ✓
The rise in the ratio could have been caused by the successful launch of a new product with high demand creating an inflated launch price	✓	
The rise in the ratio could have been due to savings in delivery fuel costs caused by reduced petrol prices.		✓

92 CRASHER

(a)

	True ✓	False ✓
Return on capital employed is calculated using figures from both the statement of profit or loss and the statement of financial position.	✓	
If a ratio reduces compared to the previous year, this will always mean that performance has deteriorated		✓
Ratios are the only way for users to analyse the performance of a business.		✓

(b) (i)

Return on capital employed (%)	16.99% (180,350 / (526,854 + 534,600))
Net profit margin (%)	13.98% (180,350 / 1,290,160)

(ii) The gross profit percentage shows **an improvement** when compared to the previous year's figures.

(c)   Scenario 1

	Increase ✓	Unchanged ✓	Decrease ✓
Cost of sales percentage			✓
Gross profit percentage	✓		

Scenario 2

	Increase ✓	Unchanged ✓	Decrease ✓
Cost of sales percentage	✓		
Gross profit percentage			✓

93   SHANNON

(a)

	True ✓	False ✓
Shannon's business' return on capital employed would increase		✓
Shannon's gross profit margin is likely to be unaffected		✓
Cost of sales/revenue percentage will increase	✓	

(b)   (i)

Return on capital employed	56.61 (75,350 / (96,200 + 54,600 – 17,690))
Gross profit margin	31.20% (146,580 / 469,760)

(ii)   The return on capital employed shows **an improvement** when compared to the previous year's figures.

(c)   Scenario 1

	Increase ✓	Unchanged ✓	Decrease ✓
Return on capital employed	✓		
Revenue		✓	

Scenario 2

	Increase ✓	Unchanged ✓	Decrease ✓
Gross profit percentage		✓	
Net profit percentage			✓

94 MAIZE

(a)

Statement	True ✓	False ✓
Gross profit margins can only increase if sales prices have increased		✓
Capital employed is calculated as capital plus current liabilities		✓
Ratios can be used to compare the performance of different businesses in the same industry	✓	
Ratios in isolation (e.g. without other ratios to provide a comparison) are not useful to the users of the financial statements	✓	

(b) (i)

Return on capital employed (%)	21.55% (52,268 / (80,223 + 162,326))
Net profit percentage (%)	12.41% (52,268 / 421,226)

(c) (ii)

Statement	True ✓	False ✓
A one-off advertising campaign that occurred in the previous year could have contributed to this increase.	✓	
The performance of the entity has deteriorated		✓

95 PARKBENCH

(a)

	True ✓	False ✓
If the cost of production increases, gross profit margin would be expected to reduce	✓	
All other things equal, increases in wages of the office and accounts staff would cause net profit margin to decrease	✓	
Users know what is going to happen to a business going forward if they utilise ratio analysis of the business' financial information		✓

(b) (i)

Return on capital employed (%)	39.11% (16,350 / (25,500 + 16,200))
Gross profit margin (%)	17.32% (26,180 / 151,160)

(ii) The selling expenses / revenue percentage shows **a deterioration** when compared to the previous year's figures.

(c) Identify what effect (if any) each of the following scenarios may have on the ratios stated.

Scenario 1

	Increase ✓	Unchanged ✓	Decrease ✓
Revenue		✓	
Gross profit percentage		✓	

Scenario 2

	Increase ✓	Unchanged ✓	Decrease ✓
Net profit percentage			✓
Cost of sales percentage	✓		

PREPARE ACCOUNTING RECORDS FROM INCOMPLETE INFORMATION

96 MULTIPLE CHOICE QUESTIONS

1 D

Trade receivables

	£		£
Balance b/d	54,550	Bank (£98,460 – £16,838)	81,622
Credit sales (bal fig)	81,632	Irrecoverable debt	2,000
		Balance c/d	52,560
	136,182		136,182

2 D

	£	£	%
Sales (100/70 × £756,000)		**1,080,000**	100
Cost of sales			
Opening Inventory	77,000		
Purchases	763,000		
Closing Inventory	(84,000)		
		(756,000)	70
		324,000	30

3 A

	£	£	%
Sales		650,000	100
Cost of sales			
Opening inventory	380,000		
Purchases	480,000		
Lost inventory (β)	**(185,000)**		
Closing inventory	(220,000)		
		(455,000)	70
Gross profit		195,000	30

4 B

	£	£
Sales		148,000
Opening inventory	34,000	
Purchases	100,000	
	134,000	
Closing inventory (β)	**(26,000)**	
Cost of sales (148,000 – 40,000)		108,000
Gross profit		40,000

5 C

$$\frac{\text{Gross profit}}{\text{Cost of sales}} \quad \frac{28{,}800}{72{,}000} = 40\%$$

	£
Sales	100,800
Cost of sales	(72,000)
Gross profit	28,800

97 A CATERING BUSINESS

(a) **Receivables ledger control account**

Balance b/d	26,000		
SDB	289,200	Bank	294,878
		Discount allowed	8,322
		Balance c/d	12,000
	315,200		315,200

(b) **VAT control**

PDB	18,800	Balance b/d	4,300
Office expenses	1,600	SDB	48,200
Bank	27,525	Cash sales	3,000
Discounts allowed (£8,322 / 6)	1,387		
Balance c/d	6,188		
	55,500		55,500

98 LOCKE TRADING

(a) **Payables ledger control account**

Bank	105,204	Balance b/d	8,700
Discounts received	3,186	PDB	112,320
Contra with RLCA	500		
Balance c/d	12,130		
	121,020		121,020

(b) **VAT control**

PDB	18,720	Balance b/d	2,300
Admin expenses	7,400	SDB	39,000
Office expenses	1,300	Discounts received (£3,186 / 6)	531
Bank	6,450		
Balance c/d	7,961		
	41,831		41,831

99 FIRST POSITION BALLET SUPPLIES

(a) £98,500

(b) **Payables ledger control account**

Bank	98,500	Balance b/d	12,400
PRDB	9,600	PDB	110,400
Discount received	4,900		
Balance c/d	9,800		
	122,800		122,800

(c) **Rent expense**

Balance b/d	300	Profit or loss	9,850
Bank	10,000	Balance c/d	450
	10,300		10,300

(d) **Electricity expense**

Bank	5,000	Balance b/d	250
Balance c/d	375	Profit or loss	5,125
	5,375		5,375

100 RELIABLE CARS

(a) £55,200

(b) **Receivables ledger control account**

Balance b/d	4,120	Bank	53,610
Credit sales	55,200	Balance c/d	5,710
	59,320		59,320

(c) £254,400

(d) **Bank account**

Balance b/d	5,630	Payroll expenses	48,000
RLCA	53,610	Administration expenses	6,400
Cash sales	254,400	Vehicle running costs	192,000
		Drawings	41,800
		VAT	17,300
		Balance c/d	8,140
	313,640		313,640

101 I.T. SOLUTIONS

(a) **Receivables ledger control account**

		Bank	49,600
		Balance c/d	6,300
Credit sales	55,900		
	55,900		55,900

(b)   **Payables ledger control account**

Bank	18,160	Purchases	22,000
Balance c/d	2,500		
Discounts received	1,340		
	22,000		22,000

(c)   **Capital account**

		Bank	16,000
		Motor vehicle cost	4,000
Balance c/d	20,000		
	20,000		20,000

102   BYRNE

(a)   **Receivables ledger control account**

Balance b/d	28,500	Bank	324,996
SDB	324,000	Sales returns	3,504
		Balance c/d	24,000
	352,500		352,500

(b)   **Payables ledger control account**

Bank	220,150	Balance b/d	23,750
Balance c/d	19,600	PDB	216,000
	239,750		239,750

(c)   **VAT control**

PDB	36,000	Balance b/d	8,300
Office expenses	1,900	SDB	54,000
Bank	26,715	Cash sales	6,000
Sales returns £3,504/6	584		
Balance c/d	3,101		
	68,300		68,300

103 PERCY

(a) £4,000

(b)

	Debit	Credit
Sales		✓
Prepayment	✓	
Loan		✓
Accrual		✓
Trade receivables	✓	

104 GROVER

(a) £5,450

(b) £57,850

(c)

	Debit	Credit	No change
Non-current assets cost		✓	
Accumulated depreciation	✓		
Trade receivables			✓
Trade payables			✓
Bank	✓		

105 CHIRON

(a) £1,000

(b) £2,200

106 PARKER

(a) £115

(b) £5,270

(c)

	Debit	Credit	No change
Non-current assets cost		✓	
Accumulated depreciation	✓		
Trade receivables			✓
Bank balance			✓
Cash balance	✓		

107 ANNABETH

£17,610

108 RUBICON

£630

Assets – Liabilities = Capital

Before £42,135 – £28,653 = £13,482

After   £43,385 – £29,273 = £14,112

Increased by £630

109 LUKE

(a) 900 + 40% = £1,260

(b) 900 × 100/60 = £1,500

110 MARK UPPS AND MARGE INNS

(a) £825 × 140/100 = £1,155

(b) £825 × 100/60 = £1,375

(c) £250 × 20/100 = £50

(d) £250 × 20/80 = £62.50

(e) £455 × 100/130 = £350

(f) £455 × 70/100 = £318.50

Section 3

MOCK ASSESSMENT QUESTIONS

THIS ASSESSMENT IS 2.5 HOURS LONG AND CONSISTS OF SIX TASKS, WHICH ALL NEED TO BE COMPLETED.

THE STANDARD VAT RATE IS 20%.

- Each task is independent. You will not need to refer to your answers to previous tasks. The total number of marks for this assessment is 120.

- Read every task carefully to make sure you understand what is required.

- Where the date is relevant, it is given in the task data.

- Both minus signs and brackets can be used to indicate negative numbers **unless** task instructions state otherwise.

- You must use a full stop to indicate a decimal point. For example, write 100.57 **not** 100,57 or 10057.

- You may use a comma to indicate a number in the thousands, but you don't have to. For example, 10000 and 10,000 are both acceptable.

TASK 1 (28 marks)

This task is about using daybooks, and accounting for and monitoring non-current assets.

(a)   (i)   Identify whether the statements below are true or false. **(3 marks)**

Statement	True ✓	False ✓
Details from credit notes received regarding a prompt payment discount will be recorded in the discounts received daybook.		
Details regarding goods sent back from customers will be recorded in the purchases returns daybook.		
A non-current asset register is a list of all of the physical items identified for future purchase by a company.		

(a)   (ii)   Identify whether the items below will qualify as revenue or capital expenditure

(4 marks)

Statement	Revenue expenditure ✓	Capital expenditure ✓
Repairs to damaged machinery in the warehouse		
An extension built on the back of the warehouse		
The installation of a new machine in the warehouse		
The cost of advertising to other companies that an existing machine owned by the company will be sold		

You are working for Teru Bogle, a sole trader with a year-end of 31 December. Teru acquired an item of plant and machinery for £60,000 on 1 January 20X2 and has been depreciation on a diminishing (reducing) balance basis at 20% per annum. Depreciation is applied on a pro-rata basis for every month the machinery is held.

Teru then sold the machinery on 31 December 20X3 for £43,200.

(b)   (i)   Calculate the depreciation that would be charged for the year ended 31 December 20X2. **(2 marks)**

£

(b)   (ii)   Calculate the depreciation that would be charged for the year ended 31 December 20X3. **(2 marks)**

£

(b) **(iii)** Complete the disposals account for the disposal of the machinery, showing clearly any amount to be transferred to the statement of profit or loss. Ensure any balancing figure is shown on the bottom row. **(8 marks)**

Disposals			
	£		£
Total		Total	

Picklist: Machinery cost, machinery accumulated depreciation, depreciation expense, statement of profit or loss, cashbook, balance b/d, balance c/d

(b) **(iv)** Complete the following sentences below, filling in the gaps where required.

(3 marks)

Teru has made a _____ on disposal of the machinery. If Teru had been offered a part-exchange against some new machinery, the part-exchange value would be recorded as a _____ in the disposals account and this would be recorded as a _____ in the machinery cost account.

Picklist: Gain, loss, debit, credit, zero, non-entry

Teru also needs to record depreciation on computer equipment for the year. Teru's computer equipment has a total cost of £25,000, acquired on 1 April 20X3. Teru believes that the computer equipment will have a useful life of 4 years, at which point it was estimated that it will have a residual value of £3,000.

(c) **(i)** Complete the journal below to account for the depreciation of the computer equipment for the year ended 31 December 20X3. **(4 marks)**

Account name	Debit £	Credit £

Picklist: Computer equipment cost, computer equipment accumulated depreciation, depreciation expense, gain/loss, disposal, depreciation liability

(c) **(ii)** Identify whether the statements below are true or false. **(2 marks)**

Statement	True ✓	False ✓
VAT can never be included in the cost of a non-current asset		
Straight-line depreciation can be calculated using a percentage or useful life		

TASK 2 (14 marks)

This task is about recording period end adjustments.

Ollie had an opening prepayment in relation to the electricity expense of £150 at 1 January 20X3 which needs to be reversed from the prepayment account in the current year. Ollie paid a further £6,500 for electricity costs during the year. This includes a £1,500 invoice relating to the three months ended 31 January 20X4.

(a) **Complete the electricity expense account for the year ended 31 December 20X3, ensuring the account is balanced off appropriately. Any balancing value should be shown on the bottom row of the account on the appropriate side.** **(8 marks)**

Electricity expense			
Detail	£	Detail	£
Total			

Picklist: Balance b/d, balance c/d, statement of profit or loss, cashbook, prepayment reversal, prepayment, accrual

Teru is looking at the final valuation of closing inventory. Teru has noted the following details in relation to some closing work-in-progress:

- Purchase cost of the raw materials: £14,000
- Labour cost applicable to the goods: £8,500
- Expected sales price of the goods: £29,300
- Estimated costs to complete the goods: £6,500

(b) (i) **Calculate the closing cost for the goods.** **(1 mark)**

£

(b) (ii) **Calculate the closing net realisable value for the goods** **(1 mark)**

£

(b) (iii) **Complete the following sentence by filling in the missing word.** **(1 mark)**

Inventory should be valued at the _____ of cost and net realisable value.

Picklist: Average, lower, higher, price

In addition to this, Teru has noted that there were some problems with credit customers during the year and has asked you about the impact of each of the following situations on the business profit for the year.

(c) **Identify the impact of each of the following situations on Teru's profit for the year ended 31 December 20X3.** **(3 marks)**

Situation	Increase profit ✓	Decrease profit ✓	No effect on profit ✓
Teru received cash from a receivable in 20X3 that was previously written off in the year to 31 December 20X2			
Teru received information that another customer has gone into liquidation			
Teru decided to reduce the allowance for irrecoverable receivables compared to last year			

TASK 3 (24 marks)

This task is about producing, adjusting, checking and extending the trial balance.

(a) **Identify where the following items would be classified in a set of financial statements.**

(3 marks)

Item	Classification
Opening inventory	
Accruals	
Gain on disposal	

Picklist: Non-current asset, current asset, income, expense, non-current liability, current liability

(b) **Identify whether the following errors will be shown by the initial trial balance or not.**

(3 marks)

Situation	Shown by trial balance ✓	Not shown ✓
An invoice for electricity of £1,000 inputted as £100.		
A cash sale correctly recorded in the bank but debited to sales		
An accrual for telephone expenses not recorded		

You are assisting with the preparation of accounts for Edi Acaster, a sole trader. A draft trial balance has been produced but this does not balance and a suspense account has been created for the difference.

After further analysis, you discovered the following errors or omissions:

- Closing inventory of £14,320 has been omitted

- An accrual of £350 was correctly recorded in the expense but credited to prepayments

- A credit sale of £1200 inclusive of VAT was all included within sales revenue

- The depreciation expense of £5,400 was credited to accumulated depreciation as £4,500

- Advertising costs of £240 were incorrectly credited to advertising expenses.

(c)   Correct the following entries by entering adjustments in the extended trial balance.

(10 marks)

	Dr £	Cr £	Adjustment Dr £	Adjustment Cr £
Capital		30,000		
Non-current assets – Cost	48,000			
Non-current assets – Acc dep'n		17,000		
Closing inventory – SFP				
Closing inventory – SPL				
Prepayments	1,320			
Accruals		530		
Trade payables		11,430		
Sales revenue		163,540		
Bank	17,430			
Rent	47,240			
Wages	31,540			
Trade receivables	6,540			
VAT		2,560		
Purchases	52,420			
Advertising expenses	8,320			
Depreciation expense	3,100			
Opening inventory	9,570			
Suspense		420		
Total	**225,480**	**225,480**		

You are also assisting in the completion of work on another client, Jian Gamble. All of the figures have been calculated but the client was unsure where to put the following items so has left them out:

- Drawings of 2,400

- Allowance for doubtful receivables of £1,250

- Cash in hand of £1,070

- Motor vehicles accumulated depreciation of £26,000

(d) **Complete the extract from the extended trial balance below. You should calculate the total profit or loss for the period and record it in the appropriate location(s).** (8 marks)

	Statement of profit or loss		Statement of financial position	
	Dr £	**Cr** £	**Dr** £	**Cr** £
Accruals				2,700
Administrative expenses	30,000			
Bank			6,640	
Capital				82,190
Cash				
Closing inventory		15,000	15,000	
Drawings				
Depreciation charge	6,600			
Motor vehicles at cost			145,000	
Motor vehicles accumulated dep'n				
Opening inventory	16,400			
Allowance for doubtful receivables				
Allowance for doubtful receivables adjustment	230			
Purchases	65,400			
Trade payables				32,500
Revenue		170,300		
Trade receivables			43,200	
Selling expenses	4,500			
VAT				6,500
Total				

TASK 4 (24 marks)

This task is about producing financial statements for sole traders and partnerships.

You have the following trial balance for a sole trader known as Handysides. All the necessary year-end adjustments have been made.

The statement of profit or loss for Handysides shows a profit of £5,400 for the period.

(a) **Prepare a statement of financial position for the business for the year ended 31 December 20X3.**   **(15 marks)**

Handysides		
Trial balance as at 31 December 20X3		
	Dr £	Cr £
Accruals		14,530
Bank	7,400	
Capital		23,000
Drawings	3,500	
Closing inventory	14,500	14,500
Depreciation charge	2,100	
General expenses	6,800	
Machinery at cost	16,400	
Machinery accumulated depreciation		7,200
Opening inventory	10,400	
Prepayments	8,200	
Purchases	49,000	
Trade payables		17,400
Rent	16,000	
Sales revenue		81,200
Trade receivables	19,430	
VAT		1,900
Wages	6,000	
	159,730	**159,730**

Handysides			
Statement of financial position as at 31 December 20X3			
	£	£	£
Non-current assets	**Cost**	**Depreciation**	**Carrying amount**
Current assets			
Current liabilities			
Net current assets			
Net assets			
Financed by:			
Opening capital			
Add:			
Less:			
Closing capital			

You have been approached to assist a partnership, the Deville Partnership, with their profit appropriation account. Guang and Ping are in partnership sharing profits equally and compiling financial statements to 31 December 20X3. They are both paid a salary of £80,000 each year. They receive both interest on their capital balances and pay interest on their drawings which are all outlined below:

	Interest on capital	Interest on drawings
	£	£
Guang	8,800	0
Ping	3,100	1,480

The profit for the year ended 31 December 20X3 is £234,000 before appropriations.

(b) Prepare the appropriation account for the partnership for the year ended 31 December 20X3. Any profit figures should be shown as positive and any losses should be shown using a minus sign as negative. All other figures should be shown as positive. If any figure is zero enter 0.   **(9 marks)**

Partnership Appropriation account for the year ended 31 December 20X3:

	Total	Guang	Ping
Profit for the year			
Add:			
Less appropriation of profits:			
Profit available for distribution			

Profit share:			
Total residual profit distributed			

TASK 5 (18 marks)

This task is about accounting principles, qualities of useful information, and interpreting financial statements using profitability ratios.

(a) Which accounting principles are being described in each scenario below?   **(4 marks)**

Scenario	Principle
Ensuring inventory is valued at the lower of cost and net realisable value	
Ensuring that all goods received by the year-end are included in inventory, whether they have been paid for or not	
Recording all money put in by the owner as capital	
Applying the same accounting policies in each accounting period	

Picklist: Accruals, going concern, business entity, materiality, consistency, prudence, money measurement

(b) Identify if each of the characteristics below is one of the fundamental qualitative characteristics or enhancing qualitative characteristics of useful financial information.

(3 marks)

Characteristic	Fundamental ✓	Enhancing ✓
Understandability		
Faithful representation		
Timeliness		

(c) Identify if the statements below are true or false. (3 marks)

Statement	True ✓	False ✓
Ratio analysis cannot be used to compare two different entities		
A decline in gross profit margin could result from an increase in advertising expenses		
Ratio analysis can be performed for the same company to compare different periods		

You have been given the following key figures produced by the computerised system of a sole trader:

Figure	£
Sales revenue	80,300
Cost of sales	43,200
Other expenses	19,200
Capital	63,000
Non-current liabilities	21,000

(d) Calculate the following items to the nearest 1 decimal place from the above information:

(4 marks)

Ratio	%
Gross profit margin	
Return on Capital Employed	

Handysides has taken out a loan of £30,000 on 27 December 20X3, which it used to acquire some machinery on the same date. The accounting policy of Handysides is to charge a full year's depreciation in the year of acquisition, and records the depreciation in its other expenses.

(e)   Identify the expected impact of the new asset and loan on the profitability ratios for Handysides for the year ended 31 December 20X3.   (4 marks)

Ratio	Increase ✓	Decrease ✓	No impact ✓
Gross profit margin			
Net profit margin			
Depreciation expense/sales revenue			
Return on capital employed			

TASK 6 (12 marks)

This task is about preparing accounting records from incomplete information.

Jevons sells two types of product, both for £240. On product A, Jevons makes a 20% gross margin. On product B, Jevons charges a mark-up on cost of 20%.

(a)   Calculate the profit (in £) made by Jevons on each product

Product	Profit £
Product A	
Product B	

(2 marks)

Jevons is also unsure of the total credit sales made in the period. Jevons started the business on 1 January 20X3 and is preparing the financial statements for the year ended 31 December 20X3. Jevons has received £43,500 from credit customers during the year, has given discounts of £1,400 and recorded a contra of £2,000 with a customer that is also a supplier. At 31 December 20X3 Jevons is owed £9,600.

(b) **Complete the receivables ledger control account below and calculate the credit sales made by Jevons for the year ended 31 December 20X3.** **(5 marks)**

Receivables ledger control account			
	£		£
Balance b/d	0		

Picklist: Balance b/d, Balance c/d, credit sales, contra, cash, discounts allowed

Jevons has a similar problem with working out the credit purchases made during the year. At 31 December 20X3 Jevons owed £7,500. Jevons recorded the contra of £2,000 in the year and paid the suppliers £28,000

(c) **Complete the payables ledger control account below and calculate the credit purchases made by Jevons for the year ended 31 December 20X3.** **(4 marks)**

Payables ledger control account			
	£		£
		Balance b/d	0

Picklist: Balance b/d, Balance c/d, credit purchases, contra, cash

Jevons had a cost of sales of £32,300 for the year ended 31 December 20X3.

(d) **Based on the answer for part (c), what was Jevons' closing inventory at 31 December 20X3?** **(1 mark)**

£

Section 4

MOCK ASSESSMENT ANSWERS

TASK 1 (28 marks)

This task is about using daybooks, and accounting for and monitoring non-current assets.

(a)   (i)   **Identify whether the statements below are true or false.**

Statement	True ✓	False ✓
Details from credit notes received regarding a prompt payment discount will be recorded in the discounts received daybook.	✓	
Details regarding goods sent back from customers will be recorded in the purchases returns daybook.		✓
A non-current asset register is a list of all of the physical items identified for future purchase by a company.		✓

(3 marks)

Feedback:

Goods sent back from **customers** would be recorded in the **sales** returns day book

The fixed asset register is a list of **existing** non-current assets held

(a)   (ii)   **Identify whether the items below will qualify as revenue or capital expenditure.**

Statement	Revenue expenditure ✓	Capital expenditure ✓
Repairs to damaged machinery in the warehouse	✓	
An extension built on the back of the warehouse		✓
The installation of a new machine in the warehouse		✓
The cost of advertising to other companies that an existing machine owned by the company will be sold	✓	

(4 marks)

Feedback: Expenditure may only be capitalised if it enhances an asset so that it can generate increased economic benefit. Repairing damaged machinery does not enhance the asset – it simply returns the asset to the state it was in before the damage.

(b) **(i)** Calculate the depreciation that would be charged for the year ended 31 December 20X2.

£12,000

(2 marks)

Feedback: £60,000 × 20% = £12,000, leaving a carrying amount of £48,000

(b) **(ii)** Calculate the depreciation that would be charged for the year ended 31 December 20X3.

£9,600

(2 marks)

Feedback: £48,000 × 20% = £9,600

(b) **(iii)** Complete the disposals account for the disposal of the machinery, showing clearly any amount to be transferred to the statement of profit or loss. Ensure any balancing figure is shown on the bottom row.

Disposals			
	£		£
Machinery cost	60,000	Machinery accumulated depreciation	21,600
		Cashbook	43,200
Statement of profit or loss	4,800		
Total	64,800	Total	64,800

(8 marks)

(b) **(iv)** Complete the following sentences below, filling in the gaps where required.

Teru has made a ___*gain*___ on disposal of the machinery. If Teru had been offered a part-exchange against some new machinery, the part exchange value would be recorded as a ___*credit*___ in the disposals account and this would be recorded as a ___*debit*___ in the machinery cost account.

(3 marks)

Feedback:

This is a gain as the entry for the profit on disposal is Debit Disposals a/c, Credit SPL

The part-exchange valuation represents the proceeds of sale (hence a credit to disposals a/c) and part of the cost of the new asset acquired (hence a debit to the machinery cost a/c)

(c) (i) Complete the journal below to account for the depreciation of the computer equipment for the year ended 31 December 20X3.

Account name	Debit £	Credit £
Depreciation expense	4,125	
Computer equipment accumulated depreciation		4,125

(4 marks)

Feedback:

The asset has only been held for 9 months this year so the depreciation charge must be pro-rated: £(25,000 cost − 3,000 RV)/4yrs × 9/12 = £4,125

(c) (ii) Identify whether the statements below are true or false

Statement	True ✓	False ✓
VAT can never be included in the cost of a non-current asset		✓
Straight-line depreciation can be calculated using a percentage or useful life	✓	

(2 marks)

Feedback:

VAT is not recoverable on certain assets (such as cars) and hence must be capitalised as part of the asset's cost

TASK 2 (14 marks)

(a) Complete the electricity expense account for the year ended 31 December 20X3, ensuring the account is balanced off appropriately. Any balancing value should be shown on the bottom row of the account on the appropriate side.

Electricity expense			
Detail	£	Detail	£
Prepayment reversal	150	Prepayment	500
Cashbook	6,500	Statement of profit or loss	6,150
Total	6,650		6,650

(8 marks)

(b) (i) Calculate the closing cost for the goods

£22,500

(1 mark)

Feedback: The cost is £14,000 + £8,500 = £22,500

(b) (ii) Calculate the closing net realisable value for the goods

£22,800

(1 mark)

Feedback: The NRV is £29,300 − £6,500 = £22,800

(b)   (iii)   Complete the following sentence by filling in the missing word.

Inventory should be valued at the _____*lower*_____ of cost and net realisable value.

(1 mark)

(c)   Identify the impact of each of the following situations on Teru's profit for the year ended 31 December 20X3

Situation	Increase profit ✓	Decrease profit ✓	No effect on profit ✓
Teru received cash from a receivable in 20X3 that was previously written off in the year to 31 December 20X2	✓		
Teru has received information that another customer has gone into liquidation		✓	
Teru has decided to reduce the allowance for irrecoverable receivables compared to last year	✓		

(3 marks)

Feedback:

Item 1: Dr Cash, Cr SPL

Item 2: Dr SPL, Cr Trade receivables

Item 3: Dr Allowance, Cr SPL

TASK 3 (24 marks)

This task is about producing, adjusting, checking and extending the trial balance.

(a)   **Identify where the following items would be classified in a set of financial statements**

Item	Classification
Opening inventory	**Expense**
Accruals	**Current liability**
Gain on disposal	**Income**

(3 marks)

Feedback: Opening inventory forms part of 'cost of sales'

(b) **Identify whether the following errors will be shown by the initial trial balance or not**

Situation	Shown by trial balance ✓	Not shown ✓
An invoice for electricity of £1,000 inputted as £100.		✓
A cash sale correctly recorded in the bank but debited to sales	✓	
An accrual for telephone expenses not recorded		✓

(3 marks)

Feedback: The trial balance will only show errors where debits do not equal credits. This is only the case with item 2

(c) **Correct the following entries by entering adjustments in the extended trial balance**

	Dr £	Cr £	Adjustment Dr £	Adjustment Cr £
Capital		30,000		
Non-current assets – Cost	48,000			
Non-current assets – Acc dep'n		17,000		900
Closing inventory – SFP			14,320	
Closing inventory – SPL				14,320
Prepayments	1,320		350	
Accruals		530		350
Trade payables		11,430		
Sales revenue		163,540	200	
Bank	17,430			
Rent	47,240			
Wages	31,540			
Trade receivables	6,540			
VAT		2,560		200
Purchases	52,420			
Advertising expenses	8,320		480	
Depreciation expense	3,100			
Opening inventory	9,570			
Suspense		420	900	480
Total	**225,480**	**225,480**	**16,250**	**16,250**

(10 marks)

Feedback:

The suspense account only arises where there has been a mismatch between the debit and credit entries. This is true of items 4 and 5.

The corrections are:

Dr Suspense £900, Cr Accumulated depreciation £900

Dr Advertising expenses £480, Cr Suspense £480

(d) Complete the extract from the extended trial balance below. You should calculate the total profit or loss for the period and record it in the appropriate location(s)

	Statement of profit or loss		Statement of financial position	
	Dr £	Cr £	Dr £	Cr £
Accruals				2,700
Administrative expenses	30,000			
Bank			6,640	
Capital				82,190
Cash			1,070	
Closing inventory		15,000	15,000	
Drawings			2,400	
Depreciation charge	6,600			
Motor vehicles at cost			145,000	
Motor vehicles – accumulated dep'n				26,000
Opening inventory	16,400			
Allowance for doubtful receivables				1,250
Allowance for doubtful receivables adjustment	230			
Purchases	65,400			
Trade payables				32,500
Revenue		170,300		
Trade receivables			43,200	
Selling expenses	4,500			
VAT				6,500
Profit for the year	62,170			62,170
Total	185,300	185,300	213,310	213,310

(8 marks)

Feedback:

The profit/loss figure is the balancing amount in the SPL columns. Being on the debit side it means income exceeds expenditure and hence this is a profit, which is shown as a credit in the SFP where it represents an increase in capital.

TASK 4 (24 marks)

(a) **Prepare a statement of financial position for the business for the year ended 31 December 20X3.**

Handysides			
Statement of financial position as at 31 December 20X3			
	£	£	£
Non-current assets	Cost	Depreciation	Carrying amount
Machinery	16,400	7,200	9,200
Current assets			
Inventory		14,500	
Receivables		19,430	
Prepayments		8,200	
Bank		7,400	
		49,530	
Current liabilities			
Trade payables	17,400		
Accruals	14,530		
VAT	1,900		
		33,830	
Net current assets			15,700
Net assets			24,900
Financed by:			
Opening capital			23,000
Add: Profit			5,400
Less: Drawings			(3,500)
Closing capital			24,900

(15 marks)

(b) Prepare the appropriation account for the partnership for the year ended 31 December 20X3. Any profit figures should be shown as positive and any losses should be shown using a minus sign as negative. All other figures should be shown as positive. If any figure is zero enter 0.

Partnership Appropriation account for the year ended 31 December 20X3:

	Total	Guang	Ping
Profit for the year	234,000		
Add:			
Interest charged on drawings	1,480	0	1,480
Less appropriation of profits:			
Salaries	160,000	80,000	80,000
Interest on capital	11,900	8,800	3,100
Profit available for distribution	63,580		
Profit share:			
Total residual profit distributed	63,580	31,790	31,790

(9 marks)

TASK 5 (18 marks)

(a) Which accounting principles are being described in each scenario below?

Scenario	Principle
Ensuring inventory is valued at the lower of cost and net realisable value	Prudence
Ensuring that all goods received by the year-end are included in inventory, whether they have been paid for or not	Accruals
Recording all money put in by the owner as capital	Business entity
Applying the same accounting policies in each accounting period	Consistency

(4 marks)

(b) Identify if each of the characteristics below is one of the fundamental qualitative characteristics or enhancing qualitative characteristics of useful financial information

Characteristic	Fundamental ✓	Enhancing ✓
Understandability		✓
Faithful representation	✓	
Timeliness		✓

(3 marks)

(c)   **Identify if the statements below are true or false**

Statement	True ✓	False ✓
Ratio analysis cannot be used to compare two different entities		✓
A decline in gross profit margin could result from an increase in advertising expenses		✓
Ratio analysis can be performed for the same company to compare different periods	✓	

(3 marks)

Feedback: Advertising expenses are recognised in operating expenses and so do not affect gross profit.

(d)   **Calculate the following items to the nearest 1 decimal place from the above information:**

Ratio	%
Gross profit margin (37,100 / 80,300)	46.2
Return on Capital Employed (17,900 /84,000)	21.3

(4 marks)

Feedback:

Gross profit = £80,300 – £43,200 = £37,100

Net profit = £37,100 – £19,200 = 17,900

Capital employed = Debt + Equity = £21,000 + £63,000 = £84,000

(e)   **Identify the expected impact of the new asset and loan on the profitability ratios for Handysides for the year ended 31 December 20X3.**

Ratio	Increase ✓	Decrease ✓	No impact ✓
Gross profit margin			✓
Net profit margin		✓	
Depreciation expense/sales revenue	✓		
Return on capital employed		✓	

(4 marks)

Feedback:

Interest on the loan is recognised after net profit and hence has no effect on any of the ratios here

The depreciation is charged to other expenses and so affects net profit but not gross profit

TASK 6 (12 marks)

(a)   Calculate the profit (in £) made by Jevons on each product

Product	Profit £
Product A	48
Product B	40

(2 marks)

Feedback:

Gross margin is a % of sales price so profit = £240 × 20 % = £48

Mark-up is a % of cost so profit = £240 × 20/120 = £40

(b)   Complete the receivables ledger control account below and calculate the credit sales made by Jevons for the year ended 31 December 20X3.

Receivables ledger control account			
	£		£
Balance b/d	0	Discounts allowed	1,400
Credit sales	56,500	Contra	2,000
		Cash	43,500
		Balance c/d	9,600
	56,500		56,500

Picklist: Balance b/d, Balance c/d, credit sales, contra, cash, discounts allowed

(5 marks)

Feedback: By entering all the figures given into the T account, the balancing figure must represent credit sales

(c)   Complete the payables ledger control account below and calculate the credit purchases made by Jevons for the year ended 31 December 20X3.

Payables ledger control account			
	£		£
Cash	28,000	Balance b/d	0
Contra	2,000	Credit purchases	37,500
Balance c/d	7,500		
	37,500		37,500

(4 marks)

Feedback: By entering all the figures given into the T account, the balancing figure must represent credit purchases

(d)   **Based on the answer for part (c), what was Jevons' closing inventory at 31 December 20X3?**

£5,200

(1 mark)

Feedback:

	£
Opening inventory	Nil
Purchases	37,500
Closing inventory (ß)	**(5,200)**
Cost of sales	32,300